A WALK ON THE WILD SIDE

The Yorkshire Wolds

Paul Amess

CONTENTS

Title Page
Introduction — 1
Humber Bridge to South Cave — 3
South Cave to Goodmanham — 40
Goodmanham to Millington — 97
Millington to Thixendale — 131
Thixendale to Wintringham — 150
Wintringham to Ganton — 184
Ganton to Filey — 205
Conclusion — 228
History Walks — 231

INTRODUCTION

I have done many long-distance walks across the north of England, and I have always made an effort to learn about the places that I have walked through. I find it truly amazing that no matter where you go in our green and pleasant land, there are thousands of years of history all around you, with some often surprising and unexpected results. All you have to do, is dig.

The Wolds Way is on my own doorstep, and like many people, I have often neglected what is on my own doorstep in favour of going further afield, with the idea that I can do the local stuff anytime. Probably like many people, anytime never comes as such, so the local region goes unexplored.

Well, in this book, I finally decided to have a wander in my own back yard, so to speak, and to see what I could find. The results surprised even me, and I learned all sorts about where I lived that I could never have imagined would be true, and I also learned that it was a lot wilder here too.

HUMBER BRIDGE TO SOUTH CAVE

The official starting point of the Wolds Way is at a bench sculpture near to the massive Humber Bridge, but the walk historically starts at Hessle Haven, a tiny harbour just a few hundred yards to the east, which is where I am starting today. This is an ancient little harbour which is still in use, yet remains very picturesque.

It has a history of smuggling going back hundreds of years, which probably continues to this day, to be honest, judging by the dodgy looking people I can see nearby. In days gone by, the place was known as Fleet and was a very important place. It was the site of the ferry that crossed the Humber, thereby linking up the religiously important towns of Beverley and Lincoln, and the route was known as The Pilgrim's Way, leading to the Shrine of St John of Beverley at the Minster there.

The Ferry Boat Inn here used to offer the chance for a departing treat when it was open, but unfortunately today I find the place boarded up, so I splosh on through the puddles towards the Bridge itself, passing the small bench sculpture just near the car park.

The bridge is pretty impressive from this viewpoint, as its span arches south to North Lincolnshire a mile or so across the water. I am proud to say that my grandfather and one of my uncles worked on this bridge. When the Queen opened it in 1981, it was, in fact, the longest suspension bridge in the world and remained so until 1998, when the industrious Japanese went one better and built the Akashi Kaikyō Bridge linking the city of Kobe with Iwaya on Awaji Island, which is not just longer but is also harder to say. Just a couple of months later, Denmark completed the Great Belt Bridge, which is also longer than the Humber Bridge, and since then there have been several others, meaning that the Humber Bridge is now not even in the top ten of longest bridges, but it is still pretty cool to look at. I am told that it still holds one claim to fame – it is still the longest suspension bridge that you can actually walk across, and I have done this myself several times. Don't try it on a windy day, though, trust me.

Talks were going on as far back as 1860 to build a bridge here, and in 1872 plans were explored to build a tunnel under the estuary but came to nothing due to the technological difficulties of building under a big gloopy splodge, as the ground here consists mainly of shale and chalk. The great recession of the 1930s killed off a further attempt to build a bridge here, and then, of course, the Second World War meant that there were other priorities. After the war, the country was financially challenged, to say the least, but in 1959 the Humber Bridge Board was formed, and construction finally began in 1972.

The statistics are impressive too, and I am told that there are 44,000 miles of suspension cables in the bridge, which apparently is enough to go around the moon six times, although why anyone would want to do that is beyond me.

The bridge was constructed by first installing the suspension arms, and then installing dozens of road sections below this, which hung on several cables. According to the plans, there were 124 of these sections, and each one weighed 140 tons, which is about the same as a blue whale, or me about a week after Christmas. During the bridge's construction, ferries would bring in the road sections, which would then be hauled up one by one on steel cables, and in one incident, some of the cables snapped, leaving the piece of road section dangling precariously above the water. I must say that this was nothing to do with either my grandfather or my uncle, and anyway, the workers managed to save the section and drag it up to its correct place, where it has remained ever since.

The bridge is designed to move, too, despite looking anything of the sort. In fact, it is built to withstand winds of up to 110 miles per hour, at which point it will move a staggering 15 feet sideways. When it is fully loaded with traffic, with around 1 ton per square foot being the maximum, the bridge's centre will drop by around 12 feet too. Finally, and I find this one a bit unbelievable, the weight of the paint on the box sections of roadway, is more than the weight of the parapets.

We owe thanks for the design of this bridge to a renowned architect called Sir Ralph Freeman. He came from a fine pedigree, with his dad, also Ralph and also a Sir, being the very guy that designed nothing less than the Sydney Harbour Bridge. Ralph junior also worked on the Forth Road Bridge, the Severn Bridge and both bridges over the Bosphorous, but the Humber Bridge is considered the pinnacle of his work and for which he is remembered. Incidentally, Ralph's son Anthony went on to follow in the family business but was tragically killed in an accident on the Vasco de Gama Bridge in Lisbon in 1998, bringing to a sad end the era of the combination of the Freeman family and bridge-building forever.

Also, quite sadly, this place has become a suicide hotspot over the years, with around 200 people making a jump over the side, either into the water or onto the road or railway lines that pass beneath this colossus. Amazingly, a handful of people have even survived the jump, which is quite bizarre when you consider that it is a 100-foot drop into fairly shallow water, and there are a couple of examples definitely worth mentioning. In 2016, one man tried to drive off the side of the bridge at 100 miles per hour and somehow survived, which is extraordinary in itself. However, way back in 2005, a mother jumped off the bridge, taking her toddler with her. She is reported to have written on herself, in permanent marker, *cause of death* along with her husband's name. An RAF helicopter was scrambled, along with a lifeboat, and astoundingly both were pulled alive from the frigid waters, after being immersed for an estimated three-quarters of an hour.

I stood now slap bang in the middle of the twin towers that support the north end of the bridge, looking south into the murky waters of the Humber. I would not, for one minute, like to be in there for any length of time, and certainly not with a child, and I wondered how bad things must be to make someone contemplate such an act.

I had once been into the Humber, as a teenager many moons ago. It had been at the height of an incredibly hot summer, and me and two of my friends had walked the considerable distance from our homes in east Hull to get here. We had gone into the water in an attempt to cool off, and

I remember as we came out a police car pulling up. The police officer in the passenger seat wound his window down and said to me how he hoped I hadn't been in the water, as it was both dangerous due to drowning but also due to pollution. Bearing in mind I was still dripping water and probably pulling fish out of my pockets at the time, I am not sure what he must have thought when I denied ever having been near the water, never mind in it. I was convinced I was going to get arrested or something, but obviously, this did not happen, and by the time I had walked home, I had once again dried out. I'm pretty sure my mum must have wondered why all of my clothes were brown, however, she never said anything as I recall. For a few weeks afterwards, I was also convinced I was going to grow an extra limb, or alternatively, something might fall off, but this thankfully never happened either, at least not that I've noticed.

There were ships ploughing up the river today, presumably on a high tide, and I wondered where they were heading. Goole was probably the most obvious answer, a small port a few miles inland, and as I recall, Britain's most inland port. I have been a few times, and there is something both quite surprising but also somewhat disconcerting about wandering through farmer's fields 50 miles from the sea, yet emerging from around a corner or out of some trees to be surprised by what are pretty big ships sticking up from behind buildings.

I continued along the chalky beach, if you can call it a beach, and passed a pub, the Country Park Inn, and decided it was probably too early to stop for a break, as I had only been walking for what was probably not even half an hour. The beach began to turn into sloppy brown mud, so I jumped onto the grassy bank to carry on, and found myself on a pretty good flat path. This seemed to continue along a huge arc of the estuary, with the railway line on its other side, and looked to be pretty good walking.

I had the path to myself today, which was a refreshing change, and found myself wishing I had brought my dog. He would definitely have enjoyed it, but would probably also have jumped into the mud head first, being the little lunatic that he was.

After a while, a train came roaring past, causing the birds to momentarily flee from the trees only to return a few seconds later. On my left, the Humber continued to flow and is, in fact, responsible for draining around a fifth of England, with the Trent, Don, Aire, Ouse and Hull being the major rivers that flow into the estuary. The muddy look of the river actually has a name, too – turbidity – and the murkier a liquid is, the higher its turbidity. Judging by the looks of it, there is probably not a liquid on the planet that has higher turbidity than the Humber, other than perhaps gravy. Although it looks disgusting, the contents of this water are incredibly vital to support the saltmarshes and mudflats, which sustain large volumes of both plant and animal life. I can personally attest to this. I have been along the banks of this river several times at dusk when I have regularly been able to witness thousands of geese flying in for the night, making their tumultuous racket as they chose a landing spot one after another.

    I carried on my slow progress along the Wolds Way, and a sign said that this was also the route of the Trans-Pennine Trail. This is a somewhat longer path which runs across England and offers an alternative coast to coast trek than other similar paths, such as the actual Coast to Coast walk or the Hadrian's Wall Path. The trail starts on the west coast of England at Southport and heads south to and then through Liverpool, then turns east passing through Widnes, Warrington and Manchester before crossing the beautiful Peak District. Next stop is Penistone, then towards Doncaster and then north where it follows the north bank of the Humber Estuary, going through the very spot where I am currently standing, before heading through Hull to Hornsea, where it abruptly stops at the North Sea. I suppose you could go on if you wanted to, but I really wouldn't recommend it. The total route is over 200 miles so should not be tackled lightly; however, I am told it is a fairly easy path, following as it does disused railway lines and canal paths, so it is definitely on my hit list.

After a while, the railway line begins to distance itself from the footpath, indicating that I must be approaching North Ferriby. Almost on this exact spot in 1937, a young man named Ted Wright had also been having something of a wander, and Ted was a bit of an amateur archaeologist. What he found changed his life and rewrote the history of this place, although he would spend almost the rest of his life trying to prove it. It was here that Ted found what eventually became known as the oldest boats ever found in Europe. Unfortunately, the war intervened, and Ted went off to fight the Germans using a tank, something which he was reputedly very good at. He remained continually interested in archaeology though and was horrified during his training when he saw tanks practising manoeuvres on the historic mound of Sutton Hoo, which he soon managed to put a stop to, and for which we should all be eternally thankful. He did periodically return to Ferriby during the war, where he somehow managed to discover another boat but was unable to excavate either site due to a lingering problem with Adolf Hitler.

After the war, he returned permanently to Ferriby to dig out his two earlier discoveries. He described it as a difficult process and one similar to getting slices of crumbly cheese out of glue and managed to have them sent to the National Maritime Museum for safe-keeping. Unfortunately, due to their boggy prison for several millennia, the boats were somewhat stinky, and quite bizarrely the trustees of the museum ordered that they be chucked in the bin because of the stench.

In 1963, Ted once again found himself digging around in the mud along this shore when he managed to find his third and arguably most important boat. As he was now a trustee of the National Maritime Museum, he managed to ensure that his latest find was spared from the bin by providing a peg for each of the other trustees, and with the advent of new dating techniques, was finally vindicated when the wood was dated back to 2030 BC, meaning of course that the boat was a staggering 4,000 years old. Just a month or two after being proved right, he passed away, presumably considerably satisfied at his life's work, as well he should be.

Indeed, just a few yards further on, I stumbled across a memorial to Ted Wright and the Ferriby Boats. It is in the form of the layout of a boat's keel, but it must be said that this is not the spot where any of the boats were found, as they actually came out of the mud further down on the shoreline.

Ferriby is where the Wolds Way leaves the Humber estuary behind for good and heads north and inland. There are several paths through the village, but today I am following the quieter one that follows a thin wood just to the west. The tide is out today, but when it is in, I imagine that the only viable route would be through the village itself, which is something to bear in mind. This point is also where we leave the Trans Pennine Trail behind, though we do join the Beverley 20, another well-known local walking route, which is not surprisingly 20 miles long and goes to Beverley.

The wood is called Long Plantation and proves to be a very picturesque little place somewhat full of dog walkers who all offer a friendly *hello* without fail, and as its name suggests, it is indeed very long. A footbridge crosses the railway line, after which the woods continue for around another half a mile, offering yet more cheery greetings from several more dog walkers of all types.

I am sure you have heard of the theory that most dogs look like their owners. On this little section of the walk, I encounter perhaps one of the most obvious examples of this that I have ever seen. It is, in fact, a well-known scientific phenomenon referred to as the *canine mini-me* phenomena.

One psychologist at the University of California even went so far as to photograph dog owners and their dogs separately in a dog park, and then asked volunteers to match up which owner went with which dog, and most people were able to match them with a greater probability than what you might think. If you have a dog yourself, take a good look at it now and then find a mirror, you might be somewhat surprised. Thinking about this, though, we have to be sensible.

The resemblance may be slight but noticeable nonetheless, and nobody is saying that there is a human being somewhere who actually looks like a Chinese Crested, reputedly the ugliest breed of dog in the world. These surely are quite bizarre animals, and if you have ever seen one, you will understand what I mean when I say that they look like a gremlin, not the cute ones but the dangerous type, that has at some point caught fire and then been fired out of a cannon at a brick wall at point-blank range, but only after being in-bred with its family for ten generations and also after it has started to go bald.

Anyway, I do tend to waffle off like this now and then, but there is a point. For coming towards me on the path was a guy with ginger hair in ponytails, which actually looked pretty cool, alongside his more or less identical red setter, whom he presumably affectionately called Doppelganger. As I passed, the dog said hello, and the guy said woof.

At the end of the wood, the sound of traffic began to build, and I guessed I was approaching the dual-carriageway that sped traffic through these beautiful hills. I crossed the road junction, which was relatively new and consisted of a couple of roundabouts, with the benefit of some footpaths, and gingerly hopped over the busy roads as required. This junction had replaced an accident blackspot, and doing this walk just 20 years ago involved putting your life in your hands at this point. I fondly remember darting across this busy road in my reckless youth, which is to all intents and purposes a motorway without being designated as such, with careless abandon, coming very close to getting hedgehogged on more than one occasion.

Beyond the final roundabout, a short path soon led back into the tranquillity of the woods, which were, in fact, a bit too tranquil for my liking. Woods are usually alive with the sounds of birds singing in the trees, critters rummaging on the forest floor, and the wind darting between the branches. This wood, however, was eerily silent. I could hear no birds or animals, and I couldn't detect any wind noise either. Once the sound of the traffic had faded away after a few yards, the place was utterly, alarmingly silent.

I remember watching a documentary on one channel or another when I was younger and had picked up one piece of advice that I have carried ever since. It was an American programme, to be honest, and it related to the pitfalls of everything that might want to hug you extremely tightly while wandering around the Rockies or Yosemite or any other place on their continent to be fair.

Snakes might lunge from beneath your feet, invisible until the last minute, and take a nasty nip which might kill you or merely leave you in severe pain for six months if you are lucky. Perhaps a bear would surprise you, or more often than not you would you surprise it, though both options would generally result in the same ending, with you being a nice tasty surprise breakfast for something extremely big and hairy. If the bears and the snakes don't get you, then perhaps the mountain lions will pounce on you as you cycle past, and rip your gizzard out, resulting in a mercifully swift death, though a still somewhat painful one. And if none of them manages to get you, there is a tiny chance that wolves would track you for a couple of days and then pounce when you least expect it.

All of these things have stuck with me over the years, and although none of these animals are to be found in our lovely little land due to our immense efficiency at making all wildlife go extinct over the last couple of thousand years, something which we proficiently continue to this day, by the way, the lesson I learned from all of these examples was as follows.

If the woods are quiet, it is for a reason. If the animals and the birds have stopped all movement and are not making any noise whatsoever, it is for a reason. And that reason is this – they are listening. Listening for what I hear you ask? Well, if you think about it, why do you ever stop to listen? If you are out walking at night and you hear a noise, what do you do? If you are in the house all alone and hear a noise that you then stop to listen for again, what does it mean? It means you are afraid, my friend. But afraid of what? Of course, it can be anything, but today certainly, all of the birds and other animals in this wood are silent, and my mind begins to race as to why that might be so.

While there are not supposed to be any animals running around our countryside that would actively hunt you down and kill you, how do we really know? There have been countless examples of sightings of big cats in our countryside, often the result of rich and eccentric people suddenly realising that the cute little jaguar cub they bought from that guy in Bradford is now clearly not entirely averse to killing and eating anyone and anything that goes near it, so they simply let it go. There have also been escapes from zoos and circuses over the years, which while being unlikely, may still result in small breeding populations dotted here and there around our merry land. Locally, examples have been quite common, so much so that it has been given a name – The Wildcat of the Wolds. It is alternately known as the Brough Beast.

I saw something myself a couple of years ago. A large, cat-like figure strode across the road in front of me as I drove from my parents' house on the east coast, and it was definitely not a dog and did not look like a deer. I have cats at home and recognised the cat-like gait instantly as it wandered without care from one side of the road to the other. Foolishly perhaps, I stopped my car while at the same time telling my little boy to stay inside as it was too dangerous. I wandered to the edge of the cornfield that I had seen it vanish into and surveyed all around me to see if I could spot anything. It may have been psychological, but I suddenly felt an immense unease and had the distinct impression that something out there was looking straight back at me, though of course, I saw nothing. Nevertheless, I jumped straight back into my car and did not stop until I got home.

Of course, no one believed me, and in fact, everyone I knew scoffed when I said what I thought I had seen. My dashcam proved to provide little evidence, picking up just a spec that could, in fact, have been a dead fly on the windscreen.

How satisfied was I then, when a few days later, the local paper printed a story repeating everything that I had said, though this time someone had also provided a video as proof. A large black cat-like creature had been seen bounding across fields heading towards the Wolds, meaning there may well be a Wildcat of the Wolds after all.

All of this came flooding uncomfortably back to me as I crept as quietly as I could through this eerie wood, and it was with a great sense of relief when I finally emerged from beneath the trees at Melton Bottom next to the quarry. The last couple of hundred yards had actually eased my worries somewhat anyway, as I found myself in more familiar territory. This was the scout camp where my friend Chris volunteered and looked after disabled scouts, and I had been here once or twice with him. Finally, after a lot of reflection, I came to the conclusion that the animals were, in fact, just being quiet because they could hear a chubby old hiker prancing straight through the middle of their home.

The quarry was busy today, with two lorries waiting to leave as I waited to cross the road. Not surprisingly, the quarry produces chalk, from deposits laid down around 80 million years ago, a time that I find impossible to comprehend, and is made from the shells and skeletons of coccoliths and foraminifera. These are both the remains of single-celled orgasms, sorry, I mean organisms, and interestingly foraminifera, which is the scientific name of one of the main creatures to make up chalk, was once identified by Herodotus as far back as the 5th century BC as making up the rocks that the Great Pyramid of Giza is built from. It appears he was mistaken though, as later on it was reckoned that what Herodotus had actually found were remains of the lentils once eaten by the workers that built the pyramids. Oops.

Anyway, I crossed the road and continued up a rough track, with a long drop down into the quarry on my right, occasionally visible through gaps in the trees. As it was winter, these gaps were quite prominent, although I imagined that the foliage would block any view of the quarry in the warmer months.

It seemed like an excessively long and arduous trek up what was, in fact, a fairly shallow hill, which probably says more about my level of fitness than anything else, but regardless, I soon found myself joining the road at the top.

It was here that I found an elderly gentleman, and he was a gentleman, emptying a plastic bin bag into the boot of his car, which is something that I will have to admit I have never before witnessed. He said hello, and I went over to, well, to be nosey if I really tell the truth.

He told me that he drives around every day putting out bin bags to encourage people to use them and not throw their rubbish in the bushes, but then he goes one step further and sorts through their rubbish to recycle whatever he can. I never asked him his name or how old he was, but he was certainly very old and was probably called Bob or Bill or Tom, or something like that. He had a thick tweed jacket on which matched his flat cap, and he had lots of little badges pinned onto his walking stick, which made me ask if he was a walker. He said he was, and showed me his stick for a closer inspection. There was pretty much a badge on there for every walk or national trail I could think of, including the Pennine Way and the West Highland Way, the Cleveland Way and Hadrian's Wall Walk. I could not see one for the Wolds Way though, and when I asked him if he had done it, he looked a bit miffed and eventually said that no, he had not, almost as if he had forgotten all about that one.

I wandered along the road and down the hill towards Welton along a lane that had skinny trees imposing themselves from both sides, and after a while, I abruptly found myself on a housing estate. The houses were pleasant enough, it's just that they were a little unexpected, as I had only ever seen the older houses on my many walks to and through Welton. At the bottom of the hill, I spied the church and one of the distinctive cream-coloured phone boxes unique to this part of the country. These confuse visitors to the area, who always want to know the story behind this seemingly odd colour choice, which is actually pretty simple.

Sir Giles Gilbert Scott designed the iconic British phone box, and it actually had many variants, though the one we are most familiar with today is the K6 and is usually best known as being painted bright red. However, in days gone by, phone boxes were, in fact, a multitude of colours including green, cream or red among others, and it simply depended on where you were in the country as to what colour they were, as there were many phone companies in the early days of telephone communications which all chose different colour schemes. As these companies merged and dwindled, most came under the ownership of the General Post Office, or GPO, which decided to paint them all red in 1935 to mark the silver jubilee of King George V. This would also make them exactly the same colour as all of their letterboxes, of course, and would mean that their workmen, as it was always men back then, would only need to carry one tin of paint.

The local phone company hereabouts, however, which was by then the only one still under the control of the local authority, simply decided to keep them as they were, which was cream and green at the time, though this has since changed to cream only, again meaning that workmen and now workwomen need only carry one tin of paint, though I bet it is a fairly big one.

There is, however, one other lesser-known difference, too. If you look at any phone box anywhere in the country, the top is also adorned with a crown to represent the monarch. This is absent from all phone boxes still controlled by what is now Kingston Communications, as in Kingston-Upon-Hull, and is said by some to represent the spirit of defiance said to be found in the city ever since the English civil war when in 1642, King Charles I was famously refused entry into the city. This lack of a crown was news to me as for a long time I had assumed them all to be identical apart from the colour, and despite living in the city all my life I had never noticed it was missing, but there you go.

Anyway, my legs were telling me it was time for a rest, so I decided to go and have a sit down at one of the benches that perch alongside the small village pond. I wandered over, found an empty spot, and promptly stuffed my face with food from my bag.

Presently, of course, the village nutter decided to come and sit next to me. I knew there was something wrong when he plonked himself down right next to me, almost sitting on my rucksack which I had placed across the bench in an unsociable and ultimately unsuccessful attempt to ward off the like of vampires, missionaries and, of course, local nutters.

He started speaking to me in some unintelligible gibberish so I just smiled and waved, nodding my head every now and then, yet I remained completely oblivious to anything and everything that he said. The strange thing is, and this is strange, but after just a few minutes of his ramblings, I began to understand him. It turns out that he simply didn't have any teeth, and this alone was making him sound like a drunken Cornish pirate with a lisp.

In fact, he was telling me about Dick Turpin, the infamous English outlaw, who while not as famous as Robin Hood, has an equally fascinating story. Although he was originally born way down in Essex, like so many sensible people, Turpin eventually made his way up to Yorkshire, which I will get to shortly.

Unfortunately, almost everything we think we know about Dick is, well, bunkum. He is famed for his midnight ride from London to York and his trusty steed Black Bess, neither of which have any basis in reality, and he was far from being any kind of Robin Hood-like figure. The London to York ride can probably be attributed to another less well-known highwayman going by the name of John Nevison, who was said to have covered the distance in 15 hours, which is about the same as it takes on a train nowadays. The myth of black Bess came about in 1834 when author Harrison Ainsworth wrote a largely fictional account of these events called Rockwood, and he added the horse into the mix just to add colour to the story.

Although it is difficult to separate fact from fiction when it comes to Turpin, there are some things that we can be pretty sure of though. For instance, he was, in fact, a butcher by trade, and joined a gang in Essex, the Gregory Gang, that robbed, burgled and stole more or less anything from anyone. Indeed, his butchery skills came in particularly useful when the gang started stealing cattle. His transgressions progressed rapidly, until one day when robbing a house, he is said to have poured boiling water over one of his victims and raped another, hardly the actions of a folklore hero. After going a step further and possibly killing his own accomplice during yet another robbery, Turpin was finally forced to flee the long arm of the law, which is how he ended up in the village where I was currently sat. On the way, though, he originally hid in Epping Forest but was seen by a servant of the keeper of the forest, one Thomas Morris. Morris tried to detain Turpin and was shot and killed for his troubles.

There is some suggestion that Turpin could have lived in nearby Brough, but legend also links him to Welton. He may have links to the Green Dragon pub just next to the pond in the village and just a few yards from where I am currently sat, as he is said to have self-defenestrated, that is to have thrown himself through one of the pub windows in order to attempt an escape, though some certainly dispute this. It is also said that he was initially captured here after shooting someone's cock, and by that, I mean a male chicken that belonged to someone else before you get any funny ideas, and he then threatened to shoot the cock's owner, too. Arrested for this apparently petty act, and giving the name of John Palmer, he was taken to Beverley where he was held in the House of Correction, something which he could have avoided had he agreed to pay a small fine that was originally offered to settle the matter.

Once in Beverley, the court looked into Palmer a bit more closely, suspicious of how he had made his money. Rightfully suspecting him of horse and cattle theft, they decided to send him to York, as the charges they were now proposing were too serious for a smaller court.

This is where Palmer made his fatal mistake that would eventually lead to his death by hanging. He wrote to his brother-in-law Pompr Rivernall telling of his new identity as Palmer; however, when Rivernall saw the postmark, he refused to pay the postage and collect the letter, saying that he knew of no one in York. In those days, it was strangely the recipient of a letter that paid the postage you see, something which when you think about it you could use to really wind someone up by sending them lots of lovely expensive letters. Anyway, being uncollected as it was, the letter was moved to Saffron Walden post office, where the postmaster, a man named James Smith, allegedly recognised Turpin's handwriting. However, it is much more likely that Smith just routinely opened uncollected letters simply because he was a bit of a nosey parker and managed to hit the jackpot with this one. Turpin asked Rivernall to back up his new identity as Palmer in the letter, but once it was in the authorities' hands, Turpin's fate was finally and fatefully sealed.

He was soon linked to many of his crimes and was sentenced to death by hanging. Turpin is said to have acted with the utmost dignity at his execution and is said to have voluntarily jumped the scaffold to his death.

We owe much of this story to a chap called Richard Bayes, who wrote a pamphlet cunningly called *A Genuine History of the Life of Dick Turpin*. Unfortunately, Bayes does not quite understand the meaning of the word *genuine* and seems to confuse the word with *money-making opportunity*. Much of what he wrote was just a sensationalized fiction designed to sell as much copy as possible. Whether or not Dick Turpin really did live, work, and kill around here is certainly open to much more debate, but I can tell you one thing, he could not have picked a nicer spot.

I bade farewell to my new found friend, who mumbled some incomprehensible mumbo-jumbo in response, having decided that it was time to carry on walking if I wanted to finish before darkness fell and the Wildcat of the Wolds once more emerged on its relentless nocturnal hunt for lost, chubby hikers.

I found myself wandering up Dale Road, past some pretty little houses that seemed to get older as I neared the end of the village, although when you think about it, they actually did, although this is not what I meant. What I meant to say is that the houses near the end of the village seemed to have been built before the others. Anyway, the road turned into a track, which passed a couple of small lakes before bending this way and that past a small cottage. Emerging into a pleasant valley, I casually walked along the edge of a very dark wood, with a vivid blackness swallowing the trunks of the trees to my left, hearing a loud snap of a branch that woke me from my daydreaming. I imagined eyes staring at me from beyond this forest, and wondered what was in there that could make such a noise. This was Welton Dale and a place I had been to many times before. Usually crowded with hikers and dog walkers, I had the place to myself today. Maybe everyone else knew something I didn't.

Half a mile later, the open valley ended, and I found myself entering the wood that I had been edging along, but thankfully it had thinned out a bit. The path was a constellation of puddles, however, which I hopped, skipped and danced over merrily until I realised a family were coming the other way and were eyeing me suspiciously. Undaunted, I gave them a cheery good morning greeting, and carried on walking as if nothing had happened, though I felt a right plonker, as you often do when caught in what really should never have to be seen by another human being, which is my awful dancing,

Through the trees, I could see some kind of old domed building off to my left. Although there did not seem to be a path that led to it, I decided to go and look anyway. I could feel branches, twigs and possibly thorns snagging on my jacket, but carried on probably somewhat recklessly until a scraping across my right cheek drew blood. I had caught myself on some kind of prickly monster bush and could feel the blood being drawn down by gravity. Using a tissue failed to stem the bleeding, so I broke a bit off and stuck it to my face like you often do when you cut yourself shaving.

When I got up close to the building, I was surprised by its grandeur. It had been built very well and seemed to be ageing without any apparent major problem. I walked around it to have a look and noted a set of steps that led up to nowhere. The building was completely sealed, and I presumed it was a folly built by some rich local landowner and probably without purpose, but this is far from the truth.

This is Raikes' Mausoleum and was built by a man called Robert Raikes around 1818. Raikes was similar to Dick Turpin in a couple of ways. He had moved up here from Essex, as had Turpin, but whereas Turpin had decided to rob people of cattle and horses and the like, Raikes decided to Rob people in a much more efficient way and became a banker.

He must have been pretty successful, as he ended up living in Welton House, which was a truly magnificent stately home, although he actually inherited the house from his wife's father. Raikes married Anne Thomas in 1789, who was the daughter of the local squire Thomas Williamson. Amazingly, at this time it was difficult if not impossible for a woman to own or inherit property, something which did not begin to be addressed until around 1870 when an Act of Parliament gave women the right to be the legal owners of any money they earned and to be able to inherit property. So, when Thomas Williamson died in 1809, the house went straight to Raikes instead of Anne, which seems completely bizarre in our modern times. Sadly, the hall was demolished in 1952, along with so many classic British stately homes that became impossibly expensive to maintain.

Anyway, Raikes had the mausoleum built to house the family after death, where they all remain to this day. There have been one or two interesting incidents though, with one being recounted by a local lad who grew up in this neck of the woods, literally. David Parker was born in the village in 1931, and regularly wandered and played in the trees around the mausoleum. He recalls that it was broken into during the First World War, and many years later he and a friend managed to get into it too. He describes lead coffins on shelves around the walls. He tells of how he and his friends saw a shadow while they were down there, which inclined them to fight each other to escape. They didn't stop running until they got home, although Parker later reckoned it had just been the shadow of a tree.

Much later, in 1962, the mausoleum was desecrated once again, though this time a skull was stolen. It was later found on the banks of the Humber and returned to its rightful place, after which the vault was permanently sealed.

It looked solid enough today, and I imagined the creepy atmosphere inside, with the coffins probably covered in cobwebs and the odd scurrying creature being the only thing that disturbed the Raikes family nowadays, and decided to move on.

Going back almost but not quite the way I had come, I was surprised to find a nicely worn track back to the main path that could probably have avoided me impaling myself on the local foliage if I had gone just a few yards further one. Regardless, what was done was done, so I turned north back onto the Wolds Way.

Crossing a track, I followed the path through a thin strip of trees towards Wauldby. This had once been a village but was now just a couple of farms, along with a church and a small lake known as Wauldby Dam. The church had been built by Anne Raikes, wife of Robert, around 1835, and was very pretty indeed. On a final note, on the philanthropy of the Raikes, Robert also paid for and had installed the four clock faces on Holy Trinity Church in Hull, which has of course now been elevated to the status of a Minster.

I followed the edges of some fields which

generally led me north, past a small wood where I could hear the occasional gunshot, and then beneath the shadow of a wind turbine, which was spinning slowly despite the apparent lack of wind today.

A farm beckoned in the distance, and as I neared, I heard the shrieks and squeals of pigs coming from within some barns. I could not decide if they were being murdered or were having sex, though I figured on the latter as the sounds just went on and on as I wandered through the farmyard.

The farm drive led to the main road, where a sharp left turn followed by an almost immediate sharp right turn had me back in the fields, but only after waiting for what seemed an age for a gap in the surprisingly heavy traffic.

Luckily, before wandering across the fields to the north, I decided to check my progress on the map and realised that I had actually come the wrong way. Just after the mausoleum, I should have turned and headed west towards Brantingham, but had instead continued north.

Whenever I go the wrong way on a walk, I usually take a pragmatic approach, shrug my shoulders, turn around, and go the correct way. There is not much point in getting angry or fussed, and anyway, I always say it is the journey that is important and not the destination. Additionally, when I am out walking by myself, there is no one to blame. However, if I had been out with my friends, I would definitely have made a big deal out of this mapping mix-up and would not have let them live it down. Well, we have to have our fun, don't we?

I spent the next half-hour retracing my steps, and soon enough, I found myself once again wandering along the track past the mausoleum, which I just about managed to glimpse through the trees. This track led to a road, and a further left turn took me past some kind of stables where I spent a moment watching horses canter around a field. They were muscly beasts and looked constrained within their small enclosure, and I imagined they would let it rip if they were given half a chance.

A gate signalled the trail turning off the road, where it ventured back into the woods but on what looked like a much better track. There were a few cars parked off the road here, so for the next mile or so I was not surprised when I encountered a whole host of people out for the day, most of them with muddy coloured dogs.

It was a proper wood for a while, but then it just turned into a thin strip of trees, before finally belching me out onto another road which was called Sprout Hill. There were certainly no sprouts, but this long straight downhill track took me quickly into Brantingham. I could have taken a short cut across the fields that led straight down to the church, but thought I would walk into the village just to have a look really. It was nice enough, but unfortunately, I was at the wrong end of it. At the other end of the village is the Triton Inn, a very fine pub indeed, and while I could have done with a lemonade, I knew full well that it would be shut, so turned around and headed towards the church.

Just before the church, there is a surprisingly big car park which was pretty busy, and the only bench I could see was taken. I decided instead to sit on the nice flat wall of the church where I could take out my little flask and enjoy a nice lukewarm coffee, as well as eat my sandwiches without having to juggle everything in my hands.

I was mid-bite and very much enjoying my sandwich when I noticed a middle-aged lady approaching me with the brow of her face set in deep furrows. She was walking straight towards me and was clearly very agitated, and I actually looked around to see if there was perhaps a tramp raking through the bin behind me or maybe even someone trying to set the thing on fire, but there was no one, only me.

She stopped a few feet short of me and just stared, with her hands on her hips. I had stopped munching on my cheese and pickle at this stage, and I think I had stopped breathing as well. I had another look behind me for any offending scallywag who might now be tipping the contents of the bin onto the freshly mown grass or perhaps even dancing on a grave or some other heinous act, but alas, it was still just me.

Disrespectful, she said, as clear as anything. *Sitting on the wall, disrespectful*, and then she just walked off. I think my mouth had now dropped open, which would not have been a pretty sight, to be honest. After a few yards, she stopped, turned around, and came back. *And you have tissue on your face*, she added, before disappearing for good in a puff of smoke. She didn't, of course, but she might as well have.

I had completely forgotten about the small patch of tissue that I had used to repair my face after my brush with a deadly thorn, and when she had gone, I gently peeled it off. I discovered that I was no longer leaking, which was good, but I remained puzzled about her other comments. I have sat on many walls in my life, and have never had an issue. Maybe it was because it was the wall of a graveyard, but I reasoned logically that the inhabitants weren't likely to be bothered by my temporary parking of oneself on top of the boundary of their eternal prison, so I reasoned that if they're not bothered, why on earth would anyone else be?

Nonplussed, I finished munching my sandwiches, enjoyed a crunchy Egremont Russet, slurped back my coffee, and bid adieu to my six-foot-under friends. Before doing so, though, I mused on one of the greatest, most amazing, yet least known crimes ever to have occurred in the archaeological world, which you may or may not be surprised to learn, happened right on this very spot. Well, perhaps not the actual spot where I am now, but certainly in Brantingham. Anyway, you know what I mean.

The story starts, as all good stories do, a very, very long time ago. In fact, we are talking Roman times, with this area, in particular, being quite popular with our Romish conquerors. One of them, *who* exactly, has been lost to time, decided to build a villa in Brantingham, but just for artistic flair, I will call him Paulus. Paulus must have had a fair bit of denarii, as his villa was equipped with exquisite mosaic floors as well as central heating and probably hot and cold running water too.

At some point, of course, and to cut a long story short, Paulus got a bit sick of Britannia, probably because it was always raining, and went back home to sunnier climes. Whatever was left of Brantingham Villa gradually fell apart or was repurposed, until eventually nature took over and swallowed whatever was left.

Fast-forward almost two thousand years, and England is in the thick of war with Nazi Germany. However, some lucky soul was wandering around what was now a disused quarry, dug a little hole, and discovered two mosaic floors, which were, of course, the remnants of Brantingham Villa, as well as evidence of a hypocaust heating system. Deciding to deal with the German problem first, the mosaics were subsequently reburied until after the war.

Fast-forward once again, this time just a smidge to 1948, and both mosaics are excavated properly, with the intention of removing them to the nearby archaeology museum in Hull. On the eve of their removal, however, something mysterious happens. Presumably, the archaeologists involved were somewhat surprised when they turned up for work the next day, all ready to move the ancient treasures, only to find one of them gone.

These are not small items, it must be remembered. The one that had been stolen was around 12 feet long by 7 feet wide and would represent a considerable logistical challenge to actually shift it, yet it vanished overnight. Not surprisingly, a close watch was put on the other mosaic until it could be secured, and this can now be seen on display at the archaeology museum in nearby Hull. You can even walk on a part of it, as it makes up part of the Roman Gallery's walkway in the museum, which does not seem like the best way to preserve an ancient treasure I must add. I have been to that museum many times, something that my children will grudgingly confirm, and had always assumed it was a replica. It never occurred to me that I was trampling on and pushing various prams and buggies across something which is, well, irreplaceable.

On this subject then, if you happen to know anyone in this area or beyond who has a surprisingly exquisite bathroom or hallway, they might well have nicked it from here. There is even a rumour that it was loaded onto an aeroplane and was in America before its loss was even detected, but this is basically just gossip.

This area is supposedly rich in Roman archaeological remains, as there used to be a major Roman town at nearby Brough, which went by the name of Petuaria. There was a harbour there, and there is even evidence of a theatre or amphitheatre, and all of this still lies beneath the rather innocuous football fields in the centre of the small town. The area is also home to the fabled Parisii people, who we will come across several times on this walk. They are basically the Celtic tribe that used to live around here before even the Romans turned up, and who I sincerely hope I am descended from. This is a fast-moving story, historically speaking at least, and the University of Hull recently announced the discovery of a lost Roman town after messing around with some geophysics equipment for a few weeks in 2018, so watch this space.

As I moved off, a gentle rain began to fall, though I did not put on my wet gear as it was not going to make me wet as such. I followed the road that snaked along the floor of the valley, with woods shrouding either side and soon came to a gate that would once again take me into the trees, with the path quickly becoming very steep. Emerging from the forest at the top, and going down a hill at the other side, it was then time to head uphill once again, skirting along the edge of the wonderfully named Woo Dale.

Passing through another farm, this one devoid of all noise and activity to the point that it looked deserted, I walked along the appropriately named Steep Hill, which offered fine views down to South Cave below, and I think I could even see my car as a tiny blue dot in the distance.

My feet were tired by now, and I was ready to stop. Today had seemed like a very long day, much longer than the mileage would suggest. I was really looking forward to a nice hot bath and could already imagine soaking my battered feet in the hot soapy water, but nonetheless, I had enjoyed being out and about in the crisp cold air.

I had not been sure about walking the Wolds Way prior to starting it, but I could honestly say that after just one day, I was well and truly hooked.

SOUTH CAVE TO GOODMANHAM

We seemed to have picked a good day to walk the second stage of the Wolds Way, between South Cave and Goodmanham, which at a distance of around 12 miles, would hopefully not be too hard on our feet.

I say we because a good friend of mine had joined me. Robin had decided to come along today, and he is someone I have walked many, many miles with, so I knew I would be in good company.

To that end, we had left Robin's car in the small car park at Goodmanham, and driven to South Cave in mine, which we left on a small side road just near to where we could easily pick up the route. The sun was shining, although it was a bit nippy, and as we got out of the car and started to put our walking shoes and jackets on, we got talking to Margaret and Liz, who had seemingly arrived here just before us, and who also had walking in mind.

They were doing a circular route though and were waiting for the third member of their group, Angela, who they said was always late. This reminded me of Andy, one of our little group, who almost always was the last to arrive and who we would patiently, and to be honest sometimes impatiently, have to wait for as he then faffed around getting ready. To be fair, though, he did have a much longer drive to get to any of our walks, and deep down, we didn't really mind, but we did enjoy winding him up.

The ladies told us that they had recently been on a nice walk around Ulrome on the east coast, which naturally led to us telling them about our recent walk from Ulrome, which had ultimately seen us end up in Lancaster, and which also resulted in my first book. Robin plugged it quite well to them, apparently, as by the end of the conversation, Liz had been on her phone and had downloaded it for her husband to read, which I think made me blush in embarrassment, though I was secretly chuffed to bits deep down inside.

Conversation over, we bade them farewell and headed off east out of the village to join the path itself. We were in for a promising day, with a good forecast and reasonable temperatures which would ensure we would neither get wet nor become all hot and sweaty as we went along, at least with a bit of luck anyway.

Cars and vans sped past us as we hobbled along the grass verge, spraying us slightly with a muddy mist, but it was not long before a left turn took us away from the road and onto possibly the muddiest path I had seen this year, which was, of course, the Wolds Way. I had not brought my hiking poles, which could be a problem I mused, but luckily Rob had two and donated one to my slippery cause as I slid from puddle to puddle. Within just a minute or so, the path became even more challenging as the flatness turned into a steep hill, and to my eye resembled a well-used rugby pitch or maybe the muddy goal of a football field after the annual monsoon football tournament.

My feet were already weighing an extra couple of stone, and even at this early stage, I had given up any and all hope of staying somewhat clean, as well as realizing my mistake at not putting my gaiters on this morning, which Robin was all too quick to point out. We plodded slowly up the hill, placing our feet down ever so carefully in order to get as much grip as possible on the sticky path, and we were both out of breath in no time at all. It is hard enough going uphill in itself, but add in a path that is trying to trip you up, and where your feet slide 6 inches down the hill every time you take a step, it makes it doubly so.

Finally, though, the path began to level out a bit, and we took advantage of a small bench at the top of the hill while our feeble bodies sorted themselves out and our hearts calmed down a bit.

We could see an unbelievably long way today to the south-west, across the Humber estuary into North Lincolnshire and probably beyond, with a couple of wind farms dominating the landscape, but we also had an excellent view immediately below us of the village that we had just left.

South Cave does not seem like much of a place when you pass through, which is maybe what makes it such a nice place to live, in that it is not bothered by hordes of people crashing it daily. I'm not sure where the name comes from, as there is certainly not a single cave to be found in the area, but it can claim to be the place where John Washington, the great-grandfather of George Washington, the 1st President of the United States, came from.

It has a nice hotel, called the Cave Castle, where an escape tunnel can be found, which ran to nearby All Saints Church and dates to sometime before 1791. John Washington lived on the Cave Castle estate, so may well have been aware of this tunnel and might even have used it. Other than these two odd facts, South Cave is, well, just a nice place to live.

Having got our breath back, it was time to move on along the ridge of the hill we had just climbed which led us to next follow the path along the side of a pleasant wood. The last of the leaves fell around us, adding another layer of slipperiness to our path, determined as it was today to bring us down by hook or by crook.

By the way, if you get the temptation to go running through this wood, then you are probably going to die, seriously. Although there is no sign of it from here, there is, in fact, a huge drop into a chalk quarry just a few feet to the north. I did have a wander through this wood a few years ago, and it was as the sun was beginning to set. As the darkness grew around me, I made my way through deep foliage, and after moving through one particularly thick bush, I found myself just 6 inches from the edge of a cliff and with the chalky ground crumbling below me, something which woke me up pretty quickly as you may well guess it would.

Chalk has been quarried here for centuries, in fact probably even longer than that. While you may wonder what use cavemen would have had for chalk, especially around here where, if you remember, there are no caves in which to draw pictures of mammoths and sabre-toothed tigers, well, it turns out that there are plenty of things you can do with the stuff.

As well as drawing pictures of mammoths in caves and large willies on blackboards at school, which by the way I was never actually convicted of as there was only circumstantial evidence, chalk can also be used by farmers to increase the pH of highly acidic soil, thus ensuring that your cabbages don't dissolve when you try to grow them in it. You can put it in your toothpaste as well, where it acts as an abrasive to scrub your teeth nice and clean and white, and in a similar but much more extreme way, you can polish metals with it too. If you're climbing El Capitan in Yosemite National Park, you can rub a bit of it onto your fingers and hands, which should mean that you are much less likely to fall to a splattery death, but that is, of course, assuming that you are at least a half-competent climber. Tailors use chalk when making suits to show which side you hang to, among other things, which confused me greatly the first time I was asked, which is usually to the left by the way. You can use it in England, or Scotland or Wales or more or less anywhere for that matter, to mark out football fields, but you cannot use it in America to mark out soccer fields. This is not because some government regulation prohibits its use there, but it is because there is no such thing as soccer and the proper name is football, so there.

Lastly, you can confuse ants with chalk and even stop them coming into your house if you have a problem with them. It is said that for some reason, ants don't like chalk and are pretty reluctant to cross it. I demonstrated this to my kids once and drew what I termed as Paul's Magical Ant Maze. I drew the maze around an ant, and for a while he sensed his way around it, feeling his way with his antennae, clearly looking a bit befuddled, until he eventually got a bit sick of the game, and just walked across it and wandered off. When I checked on this then, it turns out that ants are not actually all that bothered by chalk in itself. However, they do briefly change their behaviour whenever they come across almost anything that disrupts their scent trail, such as a line drawn with chalk, or Dame Judi Dench having a picnic, so there you go. It is, however, a lot easier to get hold of a piece of chalk to draw some ant defences near your door than it is to get hold of Judi Dench and persuade her to guard your house against frenzied Formicidae, which turns out to be the fancy word for ants and is pretty hard to pronounce as well.

As for the landscape itself, we will see as we go along that this area is a warren of dales and hills, and because of the chalk, water drains really well which means that there are not that many lakes around these parts. This part of the Wolds rises on the north bank of the Humber estuary, where we started of course, and bends in a huge arc first north and then east, falling into the sea at the majestic chalk cliffs in and around Flamborough Head. These are, in fact, the most northerly chalk hills in England, so there you go.

We followed the edge of the wood, heading northeast, which was Little Wold plantation, a name which belied the big hill we had just climbed, but thankfully the gradient of the hill gradually lessened as we slowly got higher, which was much welcome news for our bodies.

At the top, a right turn led us off the slippery path onto a much better track, although we did initially turn left and continue on for a few feet until we realized our mistake. Surprisingly, it was along this little track that we stumbled across a vineyard, which was possibly on the list of the things that I thought least likely to see today, along with Claudia Schiffer or the abominable snowman.

The vineyard is owned by a local farming family who decided, quite bravely in my opinion, to start the enterprise from scratch a few years ago after a holiday to South Africa, famous of course for its fine wines. The family had done traditional farming, which included chickens, pigs and crops over the years, but as the market shifted, they decided to aim higher. Although this little part of the north of England does not have quite the same type of climate as the bottom of Africa, it does, in fact, have one that is surprisingly conducive to the growing of grapes, and good grapes at that.

They started planting by hand in 2012, putting in thousands of vines that then had to sit there for years to establish themselves, and the first couple of years' worth of grapes had to be chucked in the bin, which is a real shame. The first useful harvest was gathered in 2014, albeit a small one, but the first real harvest did not come until 2016, though it was apparently well worth the wait. They haven't looked back since, and now produce a variety of wines with all of their names based on something to do with the farm, with my favourite being Chalk Hill White, which I will be hoping to try at some point. Today, though, the vines looked like mere twigs sticking out of the ground, but it was the middle of winter, so there you go.

The vineyard's location in this tiny valley is a truly magical surprise, and judging by the marquee and other tent-like structures, it looks like they do weddings or events here too, so presumably, other people must think so as well.

We moved on along the track and turned left through a gate, and while we thought that we had been on the slippiest path already today, it was in fact now that we found ourselves on it. Although not as muddy, the wet grass and the angle of the path made it treacherous, as Rob and myself found out as we slipped and slid along it. We had been chatting about something or other and didn't anticipate this bit of the path being much of a problem as it was basically just grass, but we both went over at exactly the same time. We slid a good few feet on our bums, which was more embarrassing than anything, as at just that moment two ladies out walking their dogs came into view, and for some reason, they both had huge grins on their faces.

One of them commented that it was a bit wet today, for which I thanked her immensely for her insight, and we continued down the hill, though not as quickly as what we had just covered the last 30 feet.

We were heading down to the bottom of a valley, where we would very briefly join the old Hull to Barnsley Railway Line, which is very oddly named as although it did indeed come from Hull, it never ever ran to Barnsley. It actually stopped near Stairfoot, around 2 miles short of the town, but seems as nobody knew where Stairfoot was, its builders just said it went to Barnsley. This was presumably something of a surprise for anyone that ever took this train to go to Barnsley, which was probably every passenger that ever used it when you think about it.

When it was built, there was already a railway line running to Hull, the one we crossed earlier near the Humber, and which was operated by the North East Railway, but this company was very negatively viewed by the people of the town who did not think it represented their interests, and even worse, thought it might have favoured Goole and Grimsby, hence the building of this line. This one was also the last substantial completely new railway built in the United Kingdon, so was a relative late-comer to the network when it opened in 1885.

There are a few tunnels through the hills along this stretch of the line, and a couple are only a short walk in either direction, so we decided to have a walk to Drewton Tunnel, which was the largest of the tunnels around here. It is also one of the longest railway tunnels in the United Kingdom and is well over a mile long.

We wandered along the quiet valley, heading east, and after half a mile or so we came to an old viaduct, which looked quite impressive even though it was clearly disused and crumbling away. I took a couple of pictures, and we carried along a bit further, and as we passed below the bridge, I wondered if a falling rock would show impressive timing by falling on Robin at the exact moment he passed under, or even worse, on me.

We both survived, though, and just a few feet further on we came to the strangely named Sugar Loaf Tunnel. Wandering in, I saw that it was not in a bad state really, though it was still clearly past its best. It was far too early in the day to see them, but there are hundreds of bats living in this and the other tunnels along the line, though what we did see was much scarier anyway.

Someone was obviously using this tunnel as a dumping ground, and atop a large pile of gravel that was bigger than a person, but only just, a large rat sat and eyed us warily. We eyed him warily, too, and a bit of a standoff developed. It must have been no more than a few seconds, but it seemed like an age, and eventually, a winner was determined, as me and Rob turned tail and ran. I had visions of hundreds of the things coming out of the shadows, intent on a quick snack of chubby hiker sushi, followed by swooping bats dive-bombing us, but after only a few seconds we were back out and into the sunshine, and had given up any hope of getting to Drewton tunnel, which was of course just beyond Sugar Loaf Tunnel.

The line had become a victim of Dr Beeching's cuts and finally closed in the 1960s with service gradually running down even before then. It had enjoyed a chequered history, with some of these tunnels being a part of that history. Although the longer tunnel at Drewton had been envisaged, the two shorter ones, Weedley and Sugar Loaf, had not, causing considerable extra and unanticipated expense. The whole thing nearly went bankrupt barely a year after opening, and a couple of high-profile accidents along the line didn't exactly help.

A train carrying a large load of fish as well as several passenger coaches crashed as it left Hull and ran into the back of an earlier train that had simply been left behind when its couplings failed and the engine pulling it had simply chuntered off, with the driver blissfully unaware of what he had left behind. Luckily, no one was seriously injured, though I imagine any crash involving fish would not have ended well regardless of injuries.

The second, and definitely far more serious incident, saw a steam engine blow up in the most literal sense of the word. On the 25 September 1907, train driver John Brook had halted his train and sent his fireman to pick up a signal token. This was a physical object that the train driver needed to have in his possession before proceeding onto a specific section of track, and was an early form of accident prevention technology. While this sort of practice is generally great at stopping trains crashing headlong into each other because the drivers were drunk, which was one of the intended purposes of these tokens, it does not, unfortunately, stop trains blowing themselves to smithereens when they have been subjected to poor maintenance for years on end. Poor John Brook was blown over 1,000 feet, and as you would expect after being blown 1,000 feet, he was soon very much and quite definitely, ever so slightly dead. His fireman must have gone out and bought a lottery ticket, or at least he would have if there had been a lottery then, as his little trip to get the token had probably saved his life.

The railway itself saved at least one life, probably many more, when Britain was hit by one of its worst winters ever in 1947. Easterly winds brought a cold snap, which is putting it mildly, that lasted from January to March. As January had initially been one of the milder ones on record, this surprised more or less everyone, with temperatures of 14° Celsius at first. On 23 January, though, it started to snow, and this continued for an amazing 55 days, a period that saw snowfall at least somewhere in the country every day. Snowdrifts grew and grew, with some up to 23 feet deep, and temperatures as low as −21° Celsius were recorded, which let's face it, would be pretty cold nowadays even with our nice snug centrally-heated and double-glazed homes. I can remember my grandparents telling me stories of the windows freezing on the inside when they were younger, and that was in a normal winter. In 1947, it was the whole sink full of water that froze, seriously. People would sit in their homes with multiple layers of clothing on, and would still be barely warm enough, which I quite frankly find completely unimaginable.

Anyway, the trains continued to plough through the monster drifts, and they proved to be a lifeline for the villagers at places around here, such as Little Weighton and South Cave. They were almost stopped though when one giant snow-drift blew over the top and brought a lot of chalk down with it into the cutting here, just as a train was passing below. The train's back end was entombed in ice, and the wagons had to be uncoupled and abandoned where they were and could only be released when the spring thaw came some weeks later. This left only one line open, which of course meant a reduced service.

There were shortages of coal that winter too, which meant that people struggled to stay warm, and which also resulted in shops being emptied of electric fires. This, in turn, crippled the national grid, resulting in the rationing of electricity, presumably causing more sinks to freeze up. Wildlife was decimated, and farmers lost almost a quarter of their cattle, with 4 million sheep dying in Wales alone.

Looking for someone to blame, the press and the public focused on a guy called Manny Shinwell, the government minister in charge of the Ministry of Fuel and Power. The problem at the time though was that it was the unions that were actually in charge, particularly the miners, and not Shinwell at all.

Shinwell had been reluctant to confront the miners prior to the winter and had let coal stocks decrease to dangerously low levels under his watch. He was eventually forced to resign after alternately trying to blame the climate and the railway system specifically, and capitalism in general, for the winter's events, though strangely he never tried to blame the miners. He was finally sacked in disgrace because of his inefficiencies in October of 1947 but then for some reason was appointed as minister for war. This was great while there wasn't actually a war on, but became a problem when one promptly started shortly after, much to everybody's surprise presumably, and particularly Shinwell's. With the outset of the Korean War then, Shinwell demanded excessively high military spending, and you may or may not be pleased to know that this is why you now have to pay NHS charges for spectacles to this very day, which had until then been made free under the newly inaugurated and much-heralded health service, which has of course since become a beloved national institution which politicians dare not touch, and quite rightly so.

Shinwell himself lived to the amazing age of 101, and perhaps even more amazingly, he remained an active member of the House of Lords more or less right up until he died, and is still the longest-lived peer ever. He married three times and not surprisingly outlived all of his wives, and perhaps also not surprisingly he chose to be buried with his first wife Fanny when he finally popped his clogs.

I tried to imagine the spectacle of steams trains puffing through this deep valley in days gone by and would have loved to have been able to have seen it. I can just imagine the trains emerging from one of the tunnels and chuffing along, under the viaduct, blasting through the snow as they forced their way through, almost like an unstoppable force. I've seen photographs of this, but they don't do it justice, but you can at least see that the snowdrifts were massive which explains why only the trains managed to get through to the villages along the line and why cars and trucks could not. The line continued to be a lifeline right up until its closure, and if it were still operating today, it would be one of the most beautiful routes in the country, so thanks a lot for that Dr Beeching.

Anyway, we had stayed here far too long, so decided to head off. The path went up a shallow hill to the north, through the trees that made up East Dale, following the valley floor. Thick woods stood on either side, but at this time of the year and with most of the leaves gone, it was possible to see through them for quite a distance.

We passed a young couple with one of those baby carriers where the child sits on your back, and a sweet little girl gave us a nice wave as we shuffled past. They seemed to be looking for something in one of their bags and had stopped to have a proper rummage, and as we passed, they pulled out a small bag of fruit which they then gave to the tiny child, who certainly seemed to enjoy the odd bit that she didn't drop.

We rounded a bend where the path got a bit steeper and stopped at a gate so we could take coats and jackets off, and so I could grab a sandwich. It was beginning to get quite warm as we walked, even though the temperature was probably in single figures, and I had been hearing and feeling my stomach rumble for the last half hour. As I fished out a sandwich, which had become ever so slightly squashed while in my rucksack, my eyes turned to Robin, who seemed to be going very pale.

He was patting down the pockets of his jacket, which he had now taken off, and he had a worried look on his face. I knew instantly what had happened, or at least thought I did and asked him if he had lost his car keys. If he had lost them, this would be a problem, as we were, of course, walking around 12 miles to his car. While I am sure we could use a brick or something to gain entry through a window, I was not sure how we would be able to start the thing, which would then be a bit of an issue presumably.

He hadn't lost them, he told me, which lifted my spirits immediately. Unfortunately, I was then brought crashing down once more when he advised me that he had, in fact, left them in my car, which to be honest was not much better than losing them.

As we were considering what to do, the couple with the child caught us up, so I moved my jacket and bag out of the way, which had been hanging on the gate. They stopped to talk to us and told us that the little girl on mum's back was called Millie.

Millie was trying to talk to us, and while she was very cute, I did not have a clue what she was going on about. I got the word hamster and thought I heard the word hoover, but that was it. Mum translated, and told us that Bobby the hamster had *escaped*, with the last word being in quotation marks courtesy of mum's hands and fingers. Mum then ran her forefinger across her neck, which I took as telling us that little Bobby was, in fact, an ex-hamster, and had presumably snuffed it, possibly up the tube of a vacuum cleaner, though I did not pursue the subject.

They told us that they were doing a circular of around 7 or 8 miles, and we told them that they had picked a fine day to do it. We also told them that we had picked a fine day to walk 12 miles to a car that we had no keys for, which at least made them laugh, though I guess they were laughing at us and not with us, for which I do not blame them one bit. We bade them goodbye as they wandered off ahead of us, as we stood there and considered our options, and I could still hear them chuckling from 50 yards away.

I generously offered to wait with the rucksacks while Rob popped back to the car, while he pointed out that popping back to the car would involve a 5-mile round trip that would take him at least an hour and a half. I accepted that while this was impractical, a fact which I think I conveyed to him pretty much immediately, I also told him that it was his problem, and quite frankly I didn't care what he did, so long as whatever he did do involved us getting into his car with a key at the end of the day and not smashing windows and sticking wires together in what would presumably be a futile attempt to start it, just before getting arrested by the plod.

Rob did what he is best at in these situations, and picked up his phone so that, once again, someone else could bail him out. Mrs Rob didn't answer, not because she was at work but probably just because she knew who was calling and didn't want to get involved in whatever he was up to today, but a second call to his son went through, whereupon Rob explained to Luke the slight problem we had, in that we were stranded 20 or so miles from home if he didn't bail us out.

After a good laugh, Luke agreed to meet us at Rob's car later that day, but we would arrange a more exact time when we had a better idea of when we would finish. All we could say now was that it would be some time that afternoon.

With our little crisis apparently solved, we put our packs back on and once again proceeded along the path, heading north and up the slight hill that was East Dale. We soon caught up with Millie and her parents, who stepped aside on the narrow path to let us pass, and who had clearly been going at a much slower speed. They were still laughing, at least on the inside, I thought to myself as we passed.

The path became very steep at the end of the valley as we climbed up towards some farmers fields. Breaking out of the woods, we considered stopping momentarily to get our breath back, but then more or less instantly decided to carry on when we figured that a stop was probably unnecessary. The gradient had flattened out, which allowed our lungs to recover naturally, and we were soon following a more or less level route, with excellent views down to the Humber estuary to the south-west. Visibility was particularly good today, and we could also see much of North Lincolnshire from up here. There were two or three power stations in the distance, along with countless wind turbines, and I found that these were definitely the dominating features of the landscape once again.

The view was still beautiful though, with the low winter sun illuminating the landscape in a soft, golden glow. The Humber snaked its way through the middle and is one of the largest estuaries in the country. For its size, the UK has a surprisingly large number of estuaries emptying into its various seas, and each of them has its own unique set of characteristics and supports a wide range of wildlife, both above and below the waterline.

Many people are aware of the sort-of-famous River Severn estuary, and its famous tidal bore that rips up the river rather dramatically, particularly at certain times of the year, but the Humber is perhaps less well-known. Many maps actually show it as the River Humber, but it is not actually a river as such, but as mentioned already, is an estuary in exactly the same way as the Wash is an estuary, which it is fair to say, nobody would consider was a river. Perhaps it is the Humber's shape, long and snake-like, which makes people think it is a river, but nonetheless, they are wrong as it is not. I have to admit that I considered it to be one for much of my life, but it is absolutely and definitively not a river, so there. I've gotten used to this idea now, but it took some getting used to, that's for sure, because when you realize that a single fundamental fact that you took for granted is actually not so, it messes with your head, and for me, this was one of those facts.

I have walked along the Humber many times, often near to the Humber Bridge, which was at one point the longest single-span suspension bridge in the world as you should already know by now unless you have skipped a few pages. The estuary is steeped in history too, and you must forgive me for I am about to go off on a tangent now, but bear with me as it is all very interesting and links this part of the world to so many others in the telling of this story.

On 24 August 1921, the R38 airship famously crashed into the choppy waters down there, though a bit further downstream towards Hull, killing nearly all of its crew of 49 people. This airship had been developed towards the end of the First World War as a military airship, but following the armistice, most of the orders for it were cancelled, and the one that was already nearly built was to be sold to the Americans instead of being kept by the British Government, who were somewhat financially challenged at that time.

The whole thing was basically rushed, as things tend to be during wartime emergencies, and even though the war was over, the trials were rushed too, as the builders wanted to sell it as soon as possible in order to get some much-needed cash.

The Americans had originally intended to obtain a couple of Zeppelins from the defeated Germans as part of wartime reparations, but our European cousins were apparently not good losers, and instead blew up whatever Zeppelins they had left before the Americans had the chance to pop round to pick them up. The clever Americans then decided that the Germans weren't getting away with it that easily, however, and simply forced them to pay for a couple from elsewhere, which is where the R38 comes in.

When the Americans found out about the soon to be cancelled R38 project, they became quite interested and came over to have a look. The R38 base was at Howden, a town just a few miles to the west and probably visible through binoculars today, and was one of the biggest military bases of its time. Trials were conducted, which revealed serious flaws that questioned the aircraft's durability, but the British made a few tweaks here and there and told everyone to keep calm and carry on.

The fatal flight left Howden heading for Norfolk on 23 August, where the airship would be tethered to a mast at another airship base at Pulham, however, when they arrived there, the place was shrouded in thick cloud, so instead the captain decided to head back out to sea to continue the trials. The R38 managed to achieve speeds of over

70 miles per hour during these trials, which you have got to admit is pretty much faster than you would expect an airship to go, and it also managed to do sharp turns at over 60 miles per hour. After spending the night at sea, the craft began to make its way back to Howden, passing to the south of Hull as it followed the Humber upstream.

Thousands of spectators had come out to watch, and it is fair to say that they all got a bit more than they bargained for. At 5.37 pm, the ship failed spectacularly, almost splitting in two, which saw men and equipment fall into the frigid waters below. Although it was August, we have to remember that this is the north of England, where water is never, ever warm.

As the structure failed, it fully split into two separate pieces, and the forward section caught fire. Although modern airships tend to use less dangerous types of gas, primarily helium, in those days, hydrogen was the only real option, but the problem with hydrogen is that it tends to go boom-boom at the slightest opportunity. Unfortunately, there were thirty-thousand kilograms of the stuff on board, which was only ever going to end one way, which is badly and quickly. Two massive explosions ensued, which blew out windows over a wide area of Hull, and which also gave the most dramatic possible ending to this spectacular sight. Of the five men who managed to survive, four of them had been in the tail section, and of the 17

Americans on board, only one survived.

Though this had been the first major airship disaster since the end of the First World War, it certainly wasn't the only one, and we have to wonder why people persevered with these death traps for so long. One notable example was the Wingfoot Air Crash in Chicago in 1919. Although the death toll was much lower, it still surely sent a message that was clearly not listened to.

The Wingfoot caught fire while over downtown Chicago, and the pilot and chief mechanic managed to use parachutes to escape to safety. A third member of the crew died when his parachute caught fire as he fell, which although clearly very bad, must have been a strange sight, while another person, Earl Davenport, his name not his title, saw his parachute get snagged underneath the airship and suffered a slow hot death, and a fifth person, a reporter, managed to parachute out only to break both his legs upon landing and later died in hospital. The airship itself crashed through the glass atrium of the Illinois Trust and Savings Bank, presumably with Earl Davenport still attached, surprising everyone inside and setting the place on fire and killing another ten people on the ground. Perhaps stories such as this are exactly why I don't like flying.

Things didn't get any better after the Wingfoot or the R38 examples, with seemingly little to no effort being made to stop the things blowing up, going down or snapping in half, or more often than not, an ingenious and rather creative combination of all three. In fact, people just seemed to get better at crashing the things, with an ever-increasing death toll being the result. I am reminded here of the definition of insanity, which is something along the lines of *doing the same thing over and over again and expecting a different result,* words which are usually accredited to none other than patent clerk and all-round genius Albert Einstein, but the airship designers were apparently not listening.

The list of accidents following the R38 disaster is both impressive and horrifying at the same time. Just a year after this hot watery incident, the *Roma,* a US Navy airship, hit power lines in Virginia, killing 34 of her crew in a fireball, with just a handful of survivors. The French did not want to be left out, so they appropriated an old Zeppelin and renamed it Dixmude, after the Battle of the Yser, an important battle in the First World War around Diksmuide that thwarted any plans the Germans had to completely occupy Belgium and meant that the plucky Belgians did actually manage to hold on to at least a sliver of their own territory for the rest of the war. Anyway, the French took their airship for a nice trip around the Mediterranean, only for it to be blown to bits, literally, when it was struck by lightning just near Sicily, killing all 52 people on board.

While these had all been military airships, with *had* being the operative word, of course, some bright spark, if you pardon the pun, floated the idea, if you pardon the pun once again, that it would be a good idea to develop them for civilian purposes. Powered flight in the form of aeroplanes was still in its infancy, as aeroplanes could only carry a few people a short distance, and only in daylight, and it was at least theoretically possible to build an airship that could carry fare-paying passengers long distances for many days. Enter the R101.

The R101 was one of a pair of British airships designed to travel to the furthest reaches of the Empire. It was an impressive design and was, in fact, the largest in the world at the time. Its sister ship, the R100, was designed and built in nearby Howden in the same hangars that gave birth to the R38, by none other than Barnes Wallis, who later became famous for bombs that bounced, notably used by the Dam Busters to destroy German dams of course.

While the R100, therefore, was to be built by private industry, the R101 was to be designed and built by the state-owned Royal Airship Works at Cardington in Bedfordshire, and they were appropriately named the *Capitalist Airship* and the *Socialist Airship* respectively. Perhaps tellingly, the Socialist Airship was deliberately designed to push the limits of technology at the time and was described by Nevil Shute, who assisted Barnes Wallis on the R100, as being extravagant and overambitious.

Completed in 1929, R101 entered trials and was deemed to have satisfactorily passed with flying colours, presumably red, white and blue, and embarked on its first (and of course last) overseas journey to Karachi in what was then India, on the evening of 4 October 1930.

It boasted impressive facilities, including 50 passenger cabins, a large dining room, and even a promenade for those foolish enough to want to take a peek five thousand feet directly downwards. Perhaps most worryingly, though, at least for something that carried 5 million cubic feet of highly explosive hydrogen, it also had a smoking room. Fear not, however, for those dappy designers had cunningly lined this room with copious amounts of the finest British asbestos, so even if the thing did catch fire, you wouldn't necessarily have to experience a surprisingly swift and astoundingly hot death, though you may still endure a much slower but still supposedly final and utterly certain death through some kind of cancer, respiratory failure, or maybe pulmonary heart disease if you are lucky, all of course linked to asbestosis.

Setting off from Cardington, the spiritual home of all British airships, the R101 headed south over the English Channel towards Paris, where it would then continue on to Egypt, or at least it should have. On board were Lord Cardington, the Secretary of State for Air; Sir William Sefton Brancker, your typical monocle clad British officer and also the Director of Civil Aviation; Reginald Colmore, the Director of Airship Development; Lieutenant-Colonel Vincent Crane Richmond, the chief designer of the R101, and Squadron Leader Frederick Michael Rope, another senior designer of the R101. Also aboard were 11 senior officials from the Royal Airship Works at Cardington, including Squadron Leaders, Majors and Wing Commanders, which was perhaps a bit reckless in hindsight, or even at the time, as they basically crammed onboard every top-level official who knew anything about airships or who had been in charge of some aspect of the government airship project.

Of course, it did not get very far, and in the early hours of 5 October, the R101 began to encounter bad weather and technical difficulties. An initial steep dive presumably alarmed the sleepy crew somewhat, enough to wake them up after which they managed to recover the aircraft. Although exactly what happened next is not certain, it was soon after this that the airship hit the ground near to the town of Beauvais, a few dozen miles north of Paris, and burst into flames immediately.

The cause has never been pinpointed for sure, but the inquest made great use of Lieutenant-Colonel Vincent Crane Richmond's personal diaries, which raised serious concerns about the hydrogen gasbags. The outer cover or skin was also a cause for concern and had previously proven to be much weaker than required, so it is highly likely that one of these components failed catastrophically, ultimately resulting in a very big bang.

After this, the British at least decided that enough was enough, that the idea would never take off (forgive me) and that was the end of the airship building programme in the UK. It had to be really, as more or less everyone who knew anything about building the things was by now buried in a communal grave at Cardington, unidentifiable as the bodies were. Thankfully, Barnes Wallis never went on that fateful ride and was able to help save our skins in the Second World War a few years later, for which we should all be extremely grateful. The sister ship to R101, the R100, was deflated and hung up in a shed for a year before being unceremoniously flattened by steam-rollers and sold for scrap. In retrospect, I imagine the people that would have crewed the R100 considered that they had had a lucky escape, as losing your jobs is infinitely preferential to being burned alive.

Although that was the end for the Brits, which of course meant no more great airship disasters here, other nations foolishly carried on regardless, and merely repeated the same mistakes of all of their predecessors. It was now time for the

Americans to nauseate in the shame of disaster, and this one was to prove to be the most disastrous of them all.

The USS Akron was launched in 1931 and did actually employ some measures to make it at least a little safer. For instance, rather than use hydrogen, which as we all know tends to go boom boom after even just a slight tickle with a discarded cigarette or spark of static from your shoes, they opted for the much safer fuel of helium, which when it leaked would not turn you into a crispy barbecue but would instead just make you sound really really funny. They also sorted out the gasbag leaking problem and introduced some kind of airtight gelatin-latex compound, for which if we visualise a giant condom, that should give you some idea of what we are dealing with. Incidentally, the Akron had an almost identical sister ship, USS Macon, so could fairly be described as a twin just like the R101.

It is perhaps surprising then, that after making the thing safer, the crazy Americans decided to use both the Akron and the Macon as floating aircraft carriers, and armed the things with five fighter planes that would be dangled below and set free, and could then fly back and hook onto an ingenious collection device after completing their mission. This was just as dangerous and crazy as it sounds, and the idea never really caught on in all senses of the term. The Akron also had a spy basket, which was basically the fuselage of a small plane that could be lowered down a very long cable indeed. This would allow the airship to remain discreetly hidden above the cloud while enabling an observer to magically appear below the cloud for a little snooping around, which must have looked incredibly odd indeed, as well as being downright dangerous in the extreme. In practice, this never worked, and the spy basket tended to blow around wildly. If you have ever been on a swing in a park and got the thing going to the point where it almost went all the way around, well that is what the spy basket did. In fact, this idea had already been tried and thrown in the bin 20 years earlier after the snazzy designers at Zeppelin came up with the hare-brained scheme after too much Schnapps, and realised that it was downright dangerous.

Anyway, on the evening of 3 April 1933, the Akron took to the skies for a mission over the Atlantic, although none of the crew had been issued with life-jackets and the airship only carried one tiny lifeboat. The crew were also unaware that they were heading into one of the most vicious storms that had been seen in 10 years, and lo and behold, sometime after midnight, the problems began. It is a familiar story, with a sudden loss of altitude followed by a recovery followed by a crash, so there are at least similarities with the fate of the R101.

Anyway, the Akron was soon in the choppy waters of the Atlantic, where it quickly broke up and disappeared forever. A passing merchant ship, presuming it had witnessed an aeroplane crashing, came to investigate and managed to recover 4 of the crew, though one of those pulled aboard was found to be already dead. Altogether, 73 people died that night. The navy itself launched a rescue mission, involving ships as well as another airship; however, this second airship also crashed resulting in the deaths of its crew as well.

There were countless other airship incidents, accidents and disaster across the world, and it would be remiss of me if I did not mention the Hindenburg crash of 1937. While this was not the deadliest airship disaster, though it still resulted in 36 deaths, it has certainly become the most famous, or perhaps infamous, and is what comes to mind nowadays when we are thinking about such things. Most people think this is because the footage was broadcast live, but that is not the case. Radio reporter Herbert Morrison was indeed at the scene and made his now-famous recording of the incident as it happened, famously calling out *Oh the Humanity* as he witnessed the explosions that engulfed the doomed craft.

This has since been regularly parodied in popular culture, including everything from the Simpsons, when a Duff Beer blimp crashes in a manner similar to the Hindenburg, to How The

Grinch Stole Christmas, where the Grinch in question can be heard shouting *Oh the Who-manity* when the Whoville Christmas tree burns down. I bet you didn't know that, did you?

Anyway, someone else filmed the inferno, and while the audio was broadcast later on the night of the disaster, it was sometime later still that this was synced with the film footage that we are all so familiar with now. This was, in fact, the first time that a recording of a news event was ever broadcast, but this style set the format forevermore and is perhaps what gave Orson Welles his idea for his infamous broadcast and somewhat evil prank of the following year when he described in detail how Martians were invading the north-east coast of America in War of the Worlds.

Anyway, the reason it went up in flames so quickly was that the Germans had gone back to using Hydrogen which was much easier to get hold of at the time, which reminds us of the R101 of course. In fact, the frame of the Hindenburg was built of duralumin, an early form of Aluminium, which is the same material as was used on the R101. When I say the same, I mean it literally, as the Zeppelin company had bought almost 5 tons of the salvaged wreck of the R101 after it was wrecked back in 1931.

Finally, Adolf Hitler had originally wanted the Hindenburg to be named after him, but the boss of the Zeppelin Company, Hugo Eckener, bravely refused to agree to this. Hitler was probably pretty much relieved at this outcome when the thing finally went up in smoke bearing Hindenburg's name rather than his own.

There have been countless other incidents and accidents since, although thankfully none have involved such a large loss of life as any of the previous examples. A few are worthy of mention, though, including the sister ship to the USS Akron, which of course was the USS Macon. This crashed in California in 1932, but amazingly only two people died, and 81 walked away uninjured. In another somewhat embarrassing incident for the US Navy, someone left a hangar door open at a place called Houma in Louisiana. During the night, a gust of wind blew three, yes, I said three, airships out of the hangar and they floated away. Obviously, it is hard to understand why they were not tied up to something with a bit of string, which let's face it would have been all that was needed, but there you go. One crashed into a tree and was later salvaged, while one hit electricity lines and disappeared in a puff of smoke, while the last one spontaneously combusted, but for unknown reasons.

More recently, a private blimp named the Jordache had what can only be described as an interesting journey in 1980. James Buza was taking his 170-foot-long gold-painted airship for a photoshoot in Manhattan when it took what he described as an *unplanned right descending turn*. What he means, of course, is that he crashed his airship. He goes on to say that he made a *controlled descent* into a rubbish dump and impaled his craft onto a pine tree, so again what he meant to say was that he crashed. This all happened for two possible and probable reasons. The first is that painting your poorly designed airship gold makes it considerably heavier and even more unstable than it had originally been, and the second is that Buza had never actually flown this airship before. Buza ultimately ended up in good company, though, as amazingly he managed to hit the ground just a few yards away from the exact spot where the Hindenburg was incinerated some 43 years before.

Even more recently, in 2012, an Israeli spy blimp (who knew that they even existed) crashed when a crop duster flew into it, presumably because the pilot didn't see the stealthy devil. And lastly, on this subject, the most recent crash involving an airship fittingly happened where it all began, at Cardington in Bedfordshire, when an experimental airship hit power lines and crashed into the airfield in 2016.

To me, though, the fact that we are still experimenting with airships after so long suggests that we have not yet, and probably never will get the hang of it, so we should maybe give them up as a bad job. I am going to finish off on this subject more or less where we started, with Einstein's quote that insanity is doing the same thing over and over again and expecting a different result. There is only one problem with this, however, which is that Einstein never said this. The quote has variously been attributed to either him, Benjamin Franklin or even Mark Twain, but again none are the real source. It actually has its origins much later, and it appears to have first appeared, so to speak, in of all places, a pamphlet relating to drug addicts, produced by Narcotics Anonymous in the USA in 1980. Go figure.

Anyway, we should probably get back to walking. I do go off sometimes like that, but I find that one thing leads to another, and before you know it, you have a very interesting story. Perhaps if the designers of the Akron, the Hindenburg, the R101 and the Roma, along with all the others, had taken a lesson from the R38, then they might have lived long and fruitful lives. Before we leave airships altogether, though, I just want to ask one question. How on earth did the Germans manage to so successfully bomb Britain with airships during the First World War, and why on earth were they so difficult to shoot down, when after the war they seemed to just blow up more or less all the time? That's a good question, you have got to admit?

We carried on walking, following the hedge along the side of a field, which slowly bent around to the north. We could hear fast-moving traffic, and soon came to the main road that led back to South Cave to the left, and towards Beverley to the right.

Just half a mile to our left, and just off the main road, there is a famous stone, named after St Augustine, although it is also known locally as St Austin's Stone. St Augustine is supposed to have visited this area and was said to have baptized and converted local heathens at the stone before the arrival of Christianity. We were not going there today though, but I went for a walk there a while back and can confirm that it is certainly a bit of an anomaly, sticking out of the side of a hill as it does.

When I got up close to it, I saw that it is full of strange holes, some of which were home to small critters which made me jump a bit when they poked themselves out, and the stone itself seems to be some kind of natural concrete, made up of all sorts, apparently, but it certainly contained a lot of flint. There is also a small cavity halfway up the stone, which is usually full of water, and this has led some people to believe that this stone is a healing stone. Next time I am ill, I will go check this out and get back to you. Lastly, this was said to be an ancient place of worship for the druids that lived in these parts, which eventually led to the modern name of nearby Drewton. Don't feel you have to rush to see this rock though, as it is probably going to be there for quite a while. Every seven years, a piece of it falls off, but then miraculously grows back again according to local folklore, which seems kind of pointless when you think about it.

We crossed the road and followed it to the east for a hundred yards or so, before coming back off it and heading north at High Hunsley Beacon. I know it was called this because a sign hung beneath it saying so. The path here became very boggy, with long tufts of grass interspersed with deep muddy puddles. After a very short while, it became easier to walk along the field's edge rather than the path, which wasn't a problem as any signs of the year's crops had long since vanished. Luckily, after just a few hundred yards, the field ended, and we found ourselves heading east on tarmac.

It was pretty bleak up here even now, on a sunny day, and I struggled to imagine being up here on a bad weather day. The wind was blowing from behind us, which was better than blowing in our faces, and we seemed to be making good progress. We passed straight through a crossroads and then turned left and off the road back onto grass and mud. This was good, as even the short distance we had just walked on tarmac had left an impression on our feet.

We were now heading more or less due north down a shallow hill and enjoyed a clear view in all directions but south. Thick fluffy clouds interspersed a deep blue sky, and before long we took a right turn which led down a steep hill into an ever-widening valley.

Unfortunately for Rob, but fortunately for me, this is when Rob's phone rang. Although he was off work today, he was sort of on-call, and he obviously felt compelled to answer it. I say this was unfortunate because the phone rang when Rob was descending the steepest part of the hill. I stopped momentarily while he spoke to whoever it was, and then figured I would rather wait at the bottom of the hill, rather than balanced on a precipice as I was now. As I was heading down, I heard a kerfuffle and turned around to see Rob sliding slowly on his bum, captured by gravity and heading rapidly to the valley floor. To his credit, he did not break his conversation one bit, and whoever was on the other end of that call had little inclination of the incline, or of what had just happened on it, other than perhaps my laughter in the background. I must admit I pulled my camera out and took a picture as well, although I didn't bother to help Rob up, but just left him to struggle one-handed while he continued his conversation, albeit now smothered in mud all across his back. Well, what are friends for?

Rob finished his call, and we had a quick check of the map to make sure we were going in the right direction. The Wolds Way is generally very well signposted, but we could not see a sign where we were now, despite this being a place where a change in direction was needed. We were indeed where we thought we were and we did indeed have to turn north, which is what we did, and which is also when we saw the signpost that we had both missed, half-hidden in a hedge.

Going north along a shallow valley that had probably been formed at the end of the last ice age, we had the place to ourselves. The going underfoot was a bit better too, which meant we could enjoy the view a bit more, rather than having to concentrate on the ground with every step we took.

After a few hundred yards, where the valley really widened out, a solitary fingerpost directed us to the left. The sign was almost comical, standing as it did in the middle of open grassland all by itself. We followed it anyway and were now well and truly in Swin Dale, an even wider shallow valley, with trees at the tops of the hills on both sides.

A lone figure approached us head-on for what seemed like a very long time, gradually getting larger and closer at what seemed like a snail's pace. The figure wore an impressive fedora and was accompanied by two red specs which darted around the stubble of the fields and occasionally disappeared into the treeline only to emerge a surprisingly long distance away.

We stopped to talk to this friendly dog walker as his out-of-control beasts enjoyed themselves immensely, and I commented on how many miles the dogs did for each one the owner covered. One of the dogs ran up to us, an Irish Setter by the looks of it, had a sniff at my feet and then cocked its leg before deciding better as its owner shouted at it. With a flash, it was gone again, back into the trees to find its brother or buddy, and we thought it wise to move on too, bidding farewell to the bloke in the hat.

Almost immediately, the roar of jets gave Rob and me a mild heart attack, as Hawk trainers barrelled down the valley at a ridiculously low height. I imagined the pilot veering left and right through the trees, so low did the aircraft look to be.

Another couple of figures then approached, this time an elderly couple by the looks of it, though they turned off up the hill and into the woods before our paths met. Rounding a gradual turn to the right, and climbing uphill as we did so, blades of wind turbines danced behind the hill ahead of us, which looked surreal and hypnotic from our point of view.

As we neared a road, where we turned right, Rob and I chatted about whether or not a railway line once ran through this place and along this route. It was flat and straight and looked unnatural and out of place in the wider environment, with some suspiciously looking trainy-type buildings to our left. I looked at a map later on when I was at home, however, and decided this was probably not so, and assumed it must have been a natural anomaly. Only much later did I find out about the extensive network of narrow-gauge railway lines that serviced the many small chalk quarries around this area and which met up with the standard gauge railway at Goodmanham.

This mini railway had been the brainchild of a guy called Douglas Richardson, whose family owned much of the land around here, and who had finally figured out how to make money from all the chalk scattered around these hills and valleys. The lines were only open for 30 years before they became unprofitable, however, and road haulage replaced the little steam trains that used to puff around these hills. The last trains were scrap trains, with the final engine, called Gertie, being used to collect as much scrap metal from this enterprise as possible, before she was also scrapped in 1936, marking the end of an era.

We followed the road to the east, and after a few hundred feet, we came to a farm, where we took advantage of the concrete foundations of a barn where we sat and enjoyed our lunch. The sun was shining, and we were pretty warm considering the low temperatures, and figured we had found ourselves a nice little sun trap. The occasional car sped past, but other than that we had the place to ourselves and we sat chatting about this and that as we tucked into sandwiches and pork pies.

I was thrilled when Rob pulled a couple of cans of Hobgoblin out of his bag and was soon enjoying mine. It was only later, when I looked at a

A WALK ON THE WILD SIDE

map, that I discovered that the hill we were about to go up was called Sober Hill, which I found quite amusing considering our beery lunch. Rob also pulled out of his bag a flask which allowed us to make a coffee and also some soup, followed by a couple of chocolate bars, and I began to wonder if I was inadvertently hiking with the male version of Mary Poppins, and wondered if he would pull a hat stand out of it next. He didn't though, which is a shame because that would have really impressed me, especially if it was a chocolate one.

Lunch over, we put our rucksacks back on and decided to tackle Sober Hill. It was certainly pretty steep, and as we left the farm behind and passed another barn, though this one much noisier as it was seemingly filled with piggies, we were soon both pretty much out of breath. I put this down to having just eaten, and to compensate, I told Rob I wasn't going to talk as we made our way up.

The last time we had been up here had been a few years earlier when a snowstorm had been chilling Britain to the bones, which froze much of the country solid. I remember it vividly. I had to leave my car on the drive for a week, unable to move what had essentially become a giant ice cube. The snowdrifts that day were around 5 feet deep and had threatened to consume Chris, one of our close friends who usually comes walking with us, and who is not very tall. He couldn't be here today due to work, but he rarely missed a chance to get out walking. At one point, Chris had stopped to demonstrate to us lesser mortals the correct way of diving into a snowdrift. He carefully took up the correct position, with legs slightly apart for balance, and placed his hands forward, bent his knees slightly, and dived straight into the snowdrift.

Unfortunately, the snowdrift wasn't a snowdrift as such but was more a block of ice. I am pretty sure that we all had the same cringe on our faces as we heard Chris' ribs crack on the rock-hard ice, and I'm pretty sure that this only lasted a nanosecond before we were all laughing at our crazy and now somewhat injured friend. We did everything that we could, which was nothing but did manage to get a nice picture of the fool.

There was none of that today, though, thankfully. It had been incredibly hard to hike up the hill through the deep snowdrifts, so I thanked my lucky stars that we did not have that to contend with that today. Things could have been worse then, and indeed they had been for a young girl called Sarah West who had travelled this way some years earlier. In March 1858, Sarah had been on her way across Newbald Wold just near here and had encountered a great snowstorm. She was buried in a drift for two days, but when she was found, she was still alive, just, and was somehow nursed back to health. I related this story to Rob and told him to stop moaning.

Presently, the gradient began to lessen, and we found ourselves getting our breath back, whereupon we had a quick conversation about our previous trip up here and Chris' unfortunate accident. Soon enough, we got to the top of the hill and enjoyed miles of views in all directions, and as a bonus, the weather was still behaving for us. We passed a wind farm and heard the gentle swish as each blade passed us by, and continued along a rough track, still heading north.

A young couple passed us going in the opposite direction and said they were heading to South Cave, exactly where we had come from. They were being followed by something that might once have been a dog but was now just a muddy mess. I have this exact same problem with my small dog. He is some kind of Shih Tzu cross and resembles an Ewok. His teeth stick out from his lower jaw, which just makes him look gormless and stupid, but he is a cute dog nonetheless, and one who enjoys cuddles, usually when you have just gotten comfy on the sofa. This can be quite alarming, especially if you are starting to fall asleep, as having a beast such as this jump on you in your dozy state is always something of a shock, no matter how many times it has already happened. His main problem, though, is his long hair. It collects everything. Leaves, mud, pine cones. I kid you not, I once even pulled a mouse out of there. And no matter how many times you cut his hair short and give him a good brush, within 24 hours he once again resembles the business end of an old mop.

Anyway, we joined a tarmac road which led us into the village of Hessleskew, according to the map. It wasn't so much a village, however, although there were a couple of houses and a farm, so we plodded on towards the main road up ahead of us.

I had anticipated having problems crossing this fast, busy road, but when we arrived at it, we didn't even have to slow our pace, never mind stop. There was no traffic whatsoever, so we sauntered across it at leisure, and I considered stopping in the middle to take a photo of the view down Market Weighton Hill to our left, but then decided that this foolish act is often how people died, so carried on instead.

The path ahead of us split into two, so after checking the map again, we took the left option, where we then saw the signpost that we really should have seen, had we bothered to have a proper look. This led us, again according to the map, into the village of Arras, but once again there was no village, but just a farm.

Nearby, but not quite on our route although definitely worth a mention, is Kiplingcotes racecourse, though this is not your traditional type of racecourse. First run in 1519, the Kiplingcotes Derby is one of the oldest horse races on the calendar and sees horses run along dangerous paths and tracks and through muddy, waterlogged fields on the third Thursday of March every year. If the race is ever not run one year, for whatever reason, then a rule states it must never be run again. This has resulted in some odd races, to say the least. In the harsh winter of 1947, which saw temperatures drop to record levels and severe snowdrifts cover this area, a solitary farmer led a horse along the course for the sole purpose of keeping the tradition going. This happened again in 2001, though for a different reason. Foot and mouth disease led to much of the countryside being closed, and again a single horse and rider kept the tradition alive. More recently, severe flooding in 2018 caused a similar solitary race, and of course, the 2020 race went into the bin completely, for what should be obvious reasons, and if you don't know why, then I'm not going to tell you. There were, however, two socially-distanced riders this time, which at least meant it could be classed as a race.

That the race has only been cancelled four times in its 500-year history, and the fact that 3 of those cancellations have been in the 21st century will probably make us modern Britons look a bit like pansies when we are eventually judged by history. After all, this race carried on through the Spanish Flu pandemic of 1918 and 1919 which killed at least 20 million people worldwide, possibly more, and even the bubonic plague in 1666, which killed a staggering 15% of the population of the country in just one summer alone. Samuel Pepys, the famous diarist, incidentally gave a famous account of the empty streets at the time of the plague, or the Black Death, as it became known, which is something that many more of us are probably able to relate closely to nowadays.

When I was researching all of this, I also read that the song *Ring a ring o' roses* was supposedly all about the black death. Just in case you were brought up in a cupboard in Greenland, the full words of the modern version, or at least the one I am familiar with, are as follows.

Ring a ring o' roses,
A pocket full of posies,
A-tishoo! A-tishoo!
We all fall down.

It was said at the time of the plague that holding flowers to your nose would protect you from catching it, and that the invariable sneezing and then falling down in the song translated exactly and specifically to illness and death. The modern version of the song does, however, cut out the last and probably most crucial word of the original song, though, which is *dead*. Quite bizarrely, when those in charge were looking for a way to encourage us all to wash our hands properly at the start of the COVID-19 pandemic, some bright spark in Downing Street actually suggested this song, though whether they did this in jest or maybe after snorting a line of smack, alas, we will never know. Thankfully, they presumably realized it was perhaps not the most appropriate one to use, and went instead for *Happy Birthday*, although it was a very close call.

Going back to the strange race that is the Kiplingcotes Derby, though, it also has some strange rules. First of all, jockeys can just turn up on the day and pay the entry fee, but they must weigh in at, at least, 10-stone. If you are lucky enough to weigh less than this, you must fill your pockets with stones, coins, fish, or whatever, until you hit that magic number. Horses of any age may be ridden, which has reportedly led in the past to retired racehorses being entered under fake names, which seems a bit extreme, particularly when you learn that the winner only gets 50 quid in prize money and gets to borrow the trophy for a year. The prize money then, will presumably not even pay for your petrol to get from wherever you have come from, so maybe riders do it merely for the prestige of winning

We have already heard that if the race is ever not held, then that is it and it can never be held again, but the last rule is perhaps the oddest. This states that whoever comes in second gets the rest of the prize money, and other than in the few odd years where the race hasn't really happened, this means that second place gets you much more cash than the winner. I can imagine jockeys comically slowing down right at the end so that they can get the extra prize money that accompanies second place.

Oh, and before we move on, it turns out that Ring a Ring o' Roses probably has nothing to do with the bubonic plague. This story only really came about after the end of the Second World War and seemed to have been accepted as fact without any proof whatsoever, so there.

A signpost took us from the back of the farm towards the east, where we figured we were finally on the last leg of today's walk down into Goodmanham. Although there was no sign of it, we could see many miles ahead and figured the village must be tucked out of sight in one of the hidden valleys up ahead of us. We walked along a hedge, chatting as we did so, and soon stumbled across an old man coming the other way.

Greg, as he introduced himself, appeared to be a proper walker. We got talking to him, and he proved to be very friendly. He was out on his own doing a circular walk and had parked somewhere near the transmitter we had passed near High Hunsley Beacon. He said he had to do a circular walk as he had nobody to drop him off, and his wife had refused to do so, but he said he didn't mind and was used to it.

When I asked him if he had managed to get in a lot of walking this year, he looked dejected and answered in the negative, although he then told us about his previous summer when he had bagged a good number of Munros up in Scotland. Bagging Munros is not something I had ever considered, although I presume I have already bagged at least 2 of them, having been up Ben Nevis and Ben Lomond one year. I prefer to walk for the simple enjoyment of getting out and about, and don't think I would enjoy it as much if I had a target, but each to their own.

We had a good, long and enjoyable chat with him, but after around 20 minutes, we figured we had better get a move on if we wanted to get back to the car before darkness on what was quite a short winter's day.

The path along the hedge seemed to go on for miles and miles, and in fact, it did, but eventually, we found ourselves walking down into the steep-sided valley that was Goodmanham Dale.

As we came down the hill, we passed through a gate, avoiding an impossibly large puddle as we did so, and found ourselves at the junction offering three choices of direction. Luckily, a sign pointed us to Goodmanham itself, which we duly followed.

In the layby was a small van, the back doors open and showing half a dozen bikes, although there seemed to be no one around. With that, a ginger head popped itself out of the window, introducing himself as Ed and the rest of him followed after opening the door. Asking him what he was doing with so many bikes, Ed said he was a checkpoint for some of his friends doing a triathlon. They were running here from the Humber Bridge, presumably along much the same route that we had just followed, and here they would swap jogging for bikes, with their next destination being York. This raised my eyebrows somewhat, and I found myself thinking that I was glad that we were nearly done for the day, and we plodded on. I wished I had asked what the next stage would be after the cycling, and shuddered at the thought of a mid-winter swim.

The road led us up a gentle hill with overgrown bushes on either side, which seemed to be acting as breeding grounds for small birds judging by the sound coming from them. The racket was tremendous, but despite looking very carefully indeed, I did not spy a single creature.

Coming across a disused railway line, we met some more hikers who told us they were walking the Hudson Way, which is a route from Market Weighton to Beverley, and one which we had recently completed ourselves. This line had an interesting history and had remained open for exactly 100 years, opening in 1865 and closing in 1965 thanks to the infernal Dr Beeching and his infamous cuts.

It is called the Hudson Way as it was built by George Hudson, an incredibly shady financier and politician who would probably end up in prison today. The truth is though that the practices he employed were commonly used by many back in his day, and it was just how business was done then. You scratch my back, and I'll scratch yours, that sort of thing.

The reason I knew a bit about Hudson was that I had come across him on one of my previous walks. When walking across England at a latitude of 54 Degrees North, Robin, Chris and I had walked past Howsham, near York, where he had been born. He was left a vast sum of money by his uncle, which enabled him to get his foot in the door with the landed gentry, after which he eventually became incredibly rich, although he had apparently been what I can only describe as a bit shady since he was a child. For instance, in 1816 he appeared before a court and was fined 12 shillings and 6 pence for bastardy, that is for being a bastard, and these are the court's words, not mine, I hasten to add.

One of his most notorious acts was to buy nearby Londesborough Hall to stop his rival George Leeman from building a competing railway along this route. He then used company funds to build a train station to serve the hall but which was really for his own private use. This, along with his other generally dodgy dealings, eventually forced him into exile abroad, which at a time of no extradition agreements, ensured his liberty until the law was changed that abolished jail terms for debtors. Some credit must be given to Hudson, however. He became known as the Railway King for his immense contribution to the country's railway network, was known as a benefactor to several charities, and without him, it is unlikely that York would be the great railway hub that it still is today.

Incidentally, just a short walk along the railway line to the left is St Helen's Well, an ancient well where I have on more than one occasion topped up my water bottle, although it is really better described as a spring than a well as such. It is also called the rag well, as evidenced by the myriad of colourful cloth always found to be hanging in the trees or tied to the fence for luck, with legend advising you to dip your rag or cloth in the water before tying it on.

St Helen was the mother of Constantine the Great, who was proclaimed Roman Emperor just up the road in York in 306 AD. She was a busy gal, even in her old age, when she went on a pilgrimage to the holy land and somehow managed to find the true cross upon which Jesus was crucified, along with the sacred nails used to crucify him. I suspect, however, that she may have been fleeced by a local Jerusalem version of George Hudson, but there you go. If you want to see the spring, you have to go up some steps from the railway line, though it can be easy to miss.

After this, the road got a bit steeper, and we both huffed and puffed, a bit like one of George

Hudson's trains, slowly and steadily up the hill. The birds continued to tweet ferociously in the bushes, still invisible to us both, with Rifle Butts Quarry, a nature reserve, to our right, which was so named as it had been a shooting range in the Second World War. When we stuck our head in, we found a shelter that had been erected to protect the quarry face, which struck me as being a bit odd, but anyway it also makes a great place for a picnic if it happens to be raining.

The road continued for a surprisingly long way, as we had previously thought we were more or less in Goodmanham itself, and it got narrower as it did so. Secreting ourselves into the bushes when a rather large tractor came trundling down the hill at considerable speed, we finally caught sight of houses which signalled our imminent finish, for which we were both more than ready. We just hoped Luke would be there waiting with the car key; otherwise, we would have a considerable walk back to my car, or at least Robin would, as there was no way I was going to pay for his mistake.

A motley collection of barns, houses and bungalows greeted us as we entered the pretty little village, along with a fine church and one of the best pubs in the area, the Goodmanham Arms. I have been to this pub on several occasions, and the manager is very friendly, and the cosy atmosphere is terrific, especially on a cold winter day when there is generally a roaring fire to greet you and warm your cockles. Sadly, the pub was closed today, so we plodded on around the corner to where we had left Rob's car. There seemed to be no sign of Luke, however, which was somewhat disconcerting, and for a moment panic set in, wondering if he was perhaps lost.

As we went into the car park, however, we heard the gentle hum of an engine, and Luke was in fact parked behind a rather large white van. I suspected he had done this deliberately, knowing his sense of humour as I do. We wandered over to say hello, and after a quick chat, we gratefully took the keys, and that was that. To his credit, Luke did wind his dad up a bit, by asking him to clarify how he had managed to find himself in the middle of nowhere with his car, but without his keys, which he clearly enjoyed doing.

All in all, this had been a perfect day. The weather had stayed nice, the walking had been gentle, and we had enjoyed it immensely, and we hadn't even gotten that muddy. I think I speak for both of us though when I say that we were definitely glad to be finished. Rob promptly dropped me back at my car, after which I went straight home, where my wife made me get straight into the bath because I was filthy.

GOODMANHAM TO MILLINGTON

We met back in the car park at Goodmanham where we had previously finished, however, the duo that was myself and Rob had now expanded into a trio that included Chris. Chris had been on many of our walks and had been walking long distances a lot longer than me, and I enjoyed hearing his stories of the various exploits and capers that he had been involved in over the years.

As we sat variously perched on car seats and bonnets changing into our walking boots, the sky opened up with a cold heavy rain, and looking around at the darkened skies to all sides, it was probable that this was going to be the theme for the day, with bitter cold thrown in for good measure. As usual, though, Chris was his usual cheery self, and I heard him telling the rain where it could go and stuff itself.

When we had finished the previous walk that saw us end up here, I did not know a lot about this village, but it turns out that it has an amazing and ancient history. I have lived in Yorkshire more or less all of my life, yet even I did not appreciate the length of time people have inhabited these hills, valleys, plains and dales.

The story of people living around here, and in fact in the entire country, begins around an amazing 950,000 years ago, which is the earliest time that stone tools have been dated to in the UK. It is unknown which species these early humans were, but they were certainly not us as such, though they were definitely still people.

Of course, at this time the country still found itself in and out of various ice ages, and it is thought that several species of humans colonised what is now our home in between the cold spells, gaps which are called interglacials. To say that life was tough for these early pioneers would be an understatement, and it is highly likely that they were not quite at the top of the food chain, if you get what I mean.

With the fluctuation of the climate over tens of thousands of years, the ice-sheets came and went, seeing off each species of human as it did so, until that is, the emergence of homo-sapiens, which means us, of course.

The oldest evidence of homo-sapiens on our little island, which wasn't actually an island then as it was connected to Europe via Doggerland, which is now at the bottom of the North Sea, is from around 40,000 years ago and was found at Kent's Cavern in Devon. This occupation seems to have been somewhat sporadic, however, and continuous occupation seems to have started only around 12,000 years ago. People often consider this period to be the end of the last ice-age, but we are in fact still in it, confirmed by that white stuff we often see covering the landscape every winter, and we are simply benefitting from a warmer interglacial cycle.

As for Yorkshire specifically, one of the oldest pieces of evidence of humans, a harpoon head found in Victoria Cave in Settle, suggests we were active in the area at least 10,000 years ago, which is truly staggering, and this leads us neatly onto the Yorkshire Wolds, which itself offers substantial evidence of human occupation through prehistory, as does Goodmanham itself.

Goodmanham, it turns out, was, in fact, the ancient home of the Parisii tribe, and was the holiest place in the Kingdom of Northumbria, so it is not surprising that a temple was built here. This was the Great Temple of Woden, the father of the gods. That temple stood here for hundreds of years, until in 627 AD after King Edwin renounced paganism, his high priest Coifi rode here on horseback, threw an axe at the door, and promptly burned the place down. Some say he rode here from York, but local tradition claims he came from nearby Londesborough, which we will be passing through a little later. The church that you can see here today is said to be built on the site of the original temple, and is ancient in its own right, with parts of it dating back over 800 years.

We are continuing our walk in a southward's direction today, although we were spoiled for choice, it must be said. There are two options for the Wolds Way around here, both of which reconnect at Londesborough. One goes north from the village, down a lane next to the church, then more or less directly to Londesborough, edging around Easthorpe hill as it does so.

We will, however, be taking the more indirect route, which will lead us into the relatively small town that is Market Weighton. I say town, but it is of a size where you are not quite sure if it is a large village or a small town, but I am assured that it is definitely a town.

Anyway, after that, the path will turn north and take us through the deserted medieval village of Towthorpe, which sounds exciting surely, before re-joining the other path at Londesborough as I have already said.

Our final destination today is Millington, and we have hired the local village hall to sleep in for the night, which also sounds exciting, as this will inevitably involve a visit to the local pub for our tea. This is because we do like to support these local businesses you see and is not because it is simply an excuse for a trip to the pub. Honest.

We head out of the village heading southwest, with rain still falling all around us. Fully kitted out with our wet gear, this should not be a problem, although I imagine if it continues, I will probably get wet feet at some point as I have not brought my gaiters. I never learn, apparently.

Chris is off ahead of us, as usual, but he stops to wait for us when he gets to a junction as he is not sure which way we are going. It's lucky he stopped, as we turned left here and headed south in order to join the disused railway line that will take us into Market Weighton itself.

The path is incredibly busy with early morning joggers, dog walkers and of course us hikers all competing for space along it. Almost immediately, we are surprised as we find ourselves entering the outskirts of the town, and after passing through a playground, we are soon in the centre.

It is a thriving and bustling market town, with lots of local independent shops, so we do the decent thing and go looking for a butchers or bakers shop where we can procure a nice selection of pork pies and the like. This is harder than expected, and after walking the length of the high street, we are only able to manage to find one that is part of a national chain, and we prefer much more local ones to be honest.

We settle instead on the Market Kitchen, which looks to be a more general shop, and all pile in, at once filling up what had been an empty space. Service is speedy and polite, and we emerge back out into the cold rain clutching our paper bags full of porky treats. After we left the shop, I noticed a blue plaque as we walked back down the high street, but more of that later.

I devour mine there and then, reasoning that if it carries on raining, a soggy pie would not be any fun, and seeing me do this, Rob and Chris do the same. We walk along the high street as we stuff our faces, getting some funny looks from the early morning shoppers, but we do not care as we are lost in the moment.

Shortly, we come across the statue of one of the most famous people to come from Market Weighton, though we will be learning about two today. This first one, however, is William Bradley and is reputed to be the tallest British man to have ever been recorded.

Bradley's mum must have had an inkling that something was not quite normal, when on the cold winter's morning of 10 February 1787, she popped him out, put him on the scales, and discovered he weighed a hefty 14 pounds. This was somewhat odd, as both of his parents were of what could be called a normal size. One of his sisters was particularly tall, though; however, she was killed in an accident in her childhood, presumably one involving a low bridge, so her exact size is not known. Bradley himself is said to have grown to a staggering 7 feet 9 inches and weighed 27 stone.

Bradley grew rapidly, and it is said that the other children at his school varied between making fun of him and being scared of him. His teacher had a habit of asking Bradley to place naughty children in the beams of the roof, and only allowed them down when they promised to behave, which is something that I think should be practised nowadays.

As an adult, Bradley did the obvious thing for a man of his size and joined a travelling freak show. He is said to have travelled with the Yorkshire Pig, which was presumably a giant animal and not, for instance, an ugly bloke, and he spent the rest of his life in such activities, bewildering and amazing adults and terrifying children with his huge form. Sadly, he died pretty young, as many outsized people tend to, and was laid to rest, presumably in one of the largest graves ever dug, in his home town of Market Weighton. He was originally buried in the grounds of All Saints' Church but was re-interred inside due to the fear of body snatchers, or Resurrection Men, as they were often called.

It is a scientific fact, by the way, that taller people tend to die younger, although no one really knows why, and has been the subject of much research and speculation. For instance, of the ten tallest people ever recorded, the oldest one died at just 56 years of age, something that will probably make Chris very happy, and make Robin tremble in his boots.

Anyway, we carried on walking, and almost immediately came across a house on our left which had a plaque also remembering Bradley, as well as a depiction of his shoe size, which was truly massive. The house itself was pretty tall, but then I would guess it had to be. On a serious note, you see, this house was said to have been designed and built specifically for Bradley, and looking at the height of the doors, this is probably true.

Before we leave Market Weighton, there is one other person who is certainly worthy of mention. Not many people have heard of Margaret Lyon or the Lyon shape, but they really should have. Margaret was born in the town in 1896 and went on to study mathematics at Cambridge University. Although she passed with flying colours, she was never awarded a degree as such, as Cambridge did not award full degrees to women until as late as 1948, shame on them.

Anyway, Margaret went on to work for the Air Ministry, but realising that this avenue held little prospects for a woman, she resigned and went travelling with her sister to Switzerland. Upon returning to the UK, she then worked for various private aircraft companies, and by the late 1920s, she found herself working at Cardington in Bedfordshire, on guess what? That's right, the R101 airship.

Fortunately for her and us, she left Cardington just six weeks before the disastrous flight to India that led to the death of most of those working on the design of the airship, and instead went off to study in the USA, where she completed her master's degree at the prestigious Massachusetts Institute of Technology, who were quite happy to award one to a woman. It was while she was here that she came up with the revolutionary Lyon shape that bears her name, which is basically the best shape that an airship can possibly be, aerodynamically speaking. This has since been used to improve the aerodynamics and therefore the efficiency of airships, and later on became the standard optimum design for submarines as well, with the first one being the American built USS Albacore, which became the example that all others would follow.

Unfortunately, Margaret then did a stint working and studying in Germany, where some of her research was probably stolen and used in submarines built by the Nazis, but we can hardly blame her for that.

Margaret was a truly outstanding individual and has lately been recognized by the people of the town in the form of the blue plaque that we saw earlier. She is buried in the cemetery in the town, although I did not know this as we passed, and if you want to, you can also pop and have a look at the USS Albacore to see what the Lyon shape is exactly, as it has since been preserved as a museum piece. When I say pop, however, I should probably mention that it is in a museum in New Hampshire in the USA, so perhaps pop is not quite the right word.

We began to walk north-west along York road, and soon enough the shops gave way to houses, which in turn gave way to fields. We turned off the road to the right as we left Market Weighton behind, and headed north along a muddy track through a farmer's field. The rain was still belting down, but surprisingly my shoes still felt dry inside. Almost immediately, we saw what looked like the remnants of the old railway line off to our right, marked by a line of trees in the distance and a barely discernible earthwork. It was easier to see where the line went off to our left, however, where a small wood had now taken over the route of the line, and beyond which would have been George Hudson's private railway station a bit further on at Shiptonthorpe.

We were not relying on a map at the moment as we pretty much knew where we were going, as the signposts were pretty good along this stretch of the walk. However, Chris surprised both Robin and me when he jumped into a puddle which was somewhat deeper than anticipated, almost disappeared, and splashed us both in copious

A WALK ON THE WILD SIDE

amounts of muddy water as he quickly extracted himself from it. Of course, we didn't help him, I mean, that would be no fun, would it?

As Chris muttered something unprintable, Rob and I carefully skirted around the pond that Chris had just swum through, and at the same time, we noticed that the rain seemed to be turning into snow. I was grateful at the time that the ground was so wet, which would presumably mean that the snow would not settle, as there is nothing worse than trudging through thick, deep snowdrifts, well, apart from swimming through ponds of course.

This stretch of the path was straight and easy to follow, and we edged along the side of the fields slowly but surely. Conversation had become minimal, and I must admit that if I could have jumped into a car and gone home at this stage, I probably would have, as it was bitterly cold.

As we plodded on, we all realised that our feet were getting bigger. The mud was full of clay along this bit of the walk, and it was accumulating very quickly on our boots and shoes. Robin was the first one to stop and try to clear some of it off, almost falling headfirst into the mud as he did so. I was going to do the same as soon as I found something to lean on such as a fence or sheep, but after about two steps, Robin's feet were once again completely caked in the stuff, so I didn't bother.

Anyway, after another half mile or so and

about an hour later, we all finally dragged ourselves out of what resembled a World War One battlefield and onto the relative safety of the road. The mud had splattered further and further up our legs as we had crossed this last field and we now all looked as if we had taken part in some kind of mud-wrestling competition. The only saving grace was that the snow was actually beginning to settle, having become considerably heavier within the last half hour.

Robin was checking his phone to see if there was any kind of signal, and I read his mind, knowing that he was thinking the same as me, which was let's go home. When his phone went back into his pocket, I knew then that this was not going to happen, and we trudged onwards. We were not, however, heading north, but had decided to detour along the road to the east, to the Wolds Way Café at the roundabout.

When we walked into the café, it was not surprisingly completely empty. This is probably because most sensible people had decided to stay home because of the foul weather, and indeed also apparently included the staff. Despite a shout of hello and a ting-ting of the bell on the counter, we seemed to have the place to ourselves.

Taking our soggy coats and jackets off, I realised we had made something of a mess on the floor, which now consisted of around 2 tons of finest Yorkshire clay. We discussed whether or not

A WALK ON THE WILD SIDE

we should go on, as outside oversized snowflakes drifted gently to the ground, which was now completely white everywhere.

With a loud bang that startled us all, a lady appeared behind the counter and looked as surprised to see us as we were to see here. She was friendly enough, though, and we soon had a steaming pot of hot tea in front of us along with some home-made scones. She told us that they had not expected many people to come in today and that we were the first, and when we apologized about the floor, she told us she had seen much worse, usually when babies were running around the place, which made me squirm a little, to say the least.

She also told us that she lived at Bishop Wilton and that she had driven through quite a lot of snow on her way into work, which surprised us as this was only a few miles away. We had checked the weather forecast the night before, which suggested snow sure enough, but as we checked again this morning, eating our scones in a nice warm café, the outlook was somewhat worse.

We had a chat about the pros and cons of either giving up or carrying on, and there were many. For instance, freezing to death wasn't on any of our bucket lists of things to do before we died, or more appropriately immediately before we died. The temperature did seem to have dropped dramatically since we had set off barely two hours before, which was certainly unusual, but on the other hand, we all had ample waterproofs, multiple layers of clothing, good footwear and everything else that we would need to walk another few miles in what was now a total whiteout.

The complication was that we had left a car at Thixendale, some miles ahead. The idea had been to walk to Millington today, spend the night in the village hall which was already booked and paid for, and then continue on to Thixendale tomorrow, collect the car, and drive back to Goodmanham for the other car. Today's stretch was quite short, only around 9 miles, with another 12 tomorrow, and I think it was this combination of 2 short days that resulted in us unanimously deciding to walk on, as well as the fact that all of our plans were already in place, so to speak.

So it was, around an hour after walking into the café as muddy tramps, we headed back out into what had magically transformed into a frozen wilderness, having put on every scrap of clothing we had.

Luckily, the snow now made it somewhat easier to tackle the once muddy fields, and within just a few minutes, our boots and shoes were all sparkly clean, although we seemed to be leaving a rather unusual trail of footprints.

A right turn away from the road finally led us towards Towthorpe, and after passing through a farm, we were soon at the site of Towthorpe village, deserted in the 1600s. It was previously thought that it was the black death that caused so many villages in this area to be deserted at this time, but this has now been disproved, and the current thinking points to agricultural changes and land redistribution. Wharram Percy is perhaps much better known as a deserted village, and indeed we will be passing through there in due course, but there are many others around here, including of course this one.

There was not much to see on the ground, so to speak, other than a few grassy snow-covered mounds in the field beside Towthorpe beck, but it was a pretty enough site anyway, particularly given its recent covering of white stuff, which continued unabated as we passed through.

We trundled along the edge of the beck, and soon crossed the road that led us into the beautiful grounds of Londesborough Park. Although it was still snowing, the place seemed to be at its best, and as a double bonus, we had it all to ourselves.

I was in the front at this stage, which was probably something of a mistake, as suddenly and without warning, I was hit multiple times with snowballs, from behind. I turned around, not amused, and saw a couple of childish blokes grinning and laughing like little school kids, and then I did the only thing I could do and returned fire. Unfortunately, Robin and Chris appeared to be some kind of marksmen, and I, well, let's just say I was not.

Londesborough Park really did look good today, and as we yomped through the ever-deepening snow, we were stunned when a herd of deer appeared just a few feet ahead of us. We stopped, and they stopped, and we simply shared a moment where we all looked into one another's souls. This probably went on for just a few seconds, but it seemed to last an age, and although it is hard to describe how I felt, it was quite simply one of those things that you will never forget.

They never ran away at the sight of us, which quite frankly is the usual reaction when both animals and people encounter us in the wilds, but the clear matriarch merely snorted softly in the crisp cold air, creating a large cloud of condensation, and then slowly wandered off, followed immediately by her herd. We watched them ebb away, treading carefully as they did through the snow, and we then carried on ourselves.

We soon came to Londesborough Hall and managed to get a really good look at it as the public footpath goes straight past it. It is a very nice house, though I imagine the heating bill is massive, and although it looks old, this is not the original home. That was demolished in 1839 by one of the later owners, William Cavendish, the 6th Duke of Devonshire in order to pay for repairs to one of his other houses, which was, in fact,

Chatsworth House. In the spirit of seeing those car stickers in the back windows of old wrecks, which say something along the lines of *my other car is a Porsche*, I found myself wondering if he had one here that said *my other house is Chatsworth*.

Although it does seem a waste to tear down such an old house, we have to remember that it was an amazing 250 years old when this happened, and was about to fall down anyway. On top of that, this decision enabled him to spend his money on Chatsworth, somewhere that has since become something of a national institution and for which we should all be eternally grateful for, if only for the fantastic Christmas Market they put on every year where you can get probably the best roast pork and stuffing sandwich in England.

Anyway, the original Londesborough Hall was built way back in 1589 by George Clifford, the 3rd Earl of Cumberland, and was by all accounts pretty nice for its time, although some attribute the house to his brother Francis. However, George Clifford actually turns out to be a bit of a character, and a lot more interesting than a dusty old house. When I was researching him, I quickly formed in my head the image of a man resembling none other than the comical Edmund Blackadder, from the second series of the programme set in Elizabethan times, which is exactly the time that Clifford lived also.

The similarities extend a lot further,

though. Lord Blackadder served as a nobleman in the court of Elizabeth I, as did the Earl of Cumberland. Clifford was a gambler and a spendthrift, as was Blackadder. Both were intelligent, charismatic and handsome, and Blackadder also spent a lot of time competing against the Queen's other courtiers, as did Clifford.

Indeed, the Marquess of Bath, who apparently disliked us uncultured northerners, wrote to the Earl of Essex saying that Clifford was the *rudest Earl by reason of his northerly bringen up,* an insult I would happily accept nowadays should it be proffered. The worst I have been called lately is *a complete p*ss head,* but I'm sure there's worse to come at some point.

Conversely, Blackadder himself managed some pretty good insults, with one of my favourites being *I curse you, and hope that something slightly unpleasant happens to you, like an onion falling on your head*. This line should have mentioned a falling potato until the producers realised that potatoes had not yet been brought back to England; hence it became an onion instead. Basically, everything that Clifford was, Blackadder was also, but even more so. They even looked alike, and I wonder if Blackadder was actually based in some small way on George Clifford, the 3rd Earl of Cumberland.

Before we leave Londesborough and its beautiful parkland, it is also worth noting that famous architect Robert Hooke also worked on the place. If you have not heard of Hooke, he was a very good friend of Sir Christopher Wren, and together they earned a fortune rebuilding London after the Great Fire of London in 1666.

History has not been kind to Hooke, however, which is probably why so few people have heard of him. He has been painted as a thief of ideas, a cad and was even described by his own biographer as being *in person, but despicable,* as well as mistrustful and jealous. This depiction of Hooke influenced writers and historians for centuries to come and is probably much the fault of Sir Isaac Newton.

Hooke and Newton had had a bit of a falling out, to say the least, probably over the inverse square law of gravity, whatever the hell that is. This falling out is something that Newton took great advantage of, particularly when Hooke became the first of the pair to die. Whatever the falling out was really about, Newton exacted a bitter revenge, and was easily able to do so in his position as President of the Royal Society, and spent much of the rest of his life in a serious effort to undermine Hooke.

That Hooke was a miserable old curmudgeon was first put into doubt with the publication of his diaries in 1935, which actually painted him as a jolly little soul. For instance, his diaries make happy references to meetings with many of his friends at coffee houses and taverns and describe his philanthropy in taking in his relatives and paying for their education, although they also revealed that in doing so, he had an affair with his niece, the filthy scoundrel. To add to this, a somewhat brighter picture of him was painted when his papers were discovered at the Royal Society in 2006, which had mysteriously vanished after his death under Sir Isaac Newton's not-so-careful care.

Regardless of his personality deficiencies, however, one thing is for sure, and that is he did a great job at Londesborough.

We ventured west through the village, with no one around other than a couple of friendly horses in the field on our right. Soon enough, we came across the church and decided to go inside for a few minutes so we could shelter from the elements.

We had the place to ourselves and found that it was surprisingly big on the inside. We didn't really warm up though, in fact, it felt colder inside than it had been outside, so we were soon on our way once again.

To our delight, it had stopped snowing when we came back out, and as we stood looking at the beautiful scene all around us, I was amazed at how quiet it was, that is until Rob farted. It wasn't just a little quiet one, either, but a long drawn out echoey dry one that must have woken up the entire village.

We carried on to the end of the road and turned right at a beautiful old cottage which led us to the edge of the village and a crossroads. Going straight across to Burnby, we were now on a country lane which proved to have no traffic and judging by the snowfall, nothing had been down here at all today as there were no tracks or footprints either. We took the opportunity to walk three abreast, something that you can't usually do when out walking, as the paths are usually either too narrow or the roads too busy, and we spent the next half hour putting the world to rights about a whole host of subjects.

This road was long and straight, and we had a good view across the plains to the west, all of which seemed to be covered under a blanket of snow. We did not see another car, in fact, until we came to the junction with another road, where a snowplough was doing its job at a surprising speed as we approached, though luckily it passed a few seconds before us meaning we didn't get turned into human snowmen.

A quick check of the map told us that we should go through Partridge Farm, which should, in fact, have been called dead rabbit farm as that was what the track seemed to be covered in. After this, we followed the bottom of the hill which was on our right, where the snow was especially deep but also delightfully fluffy having just fallen, and for a minute I considered building maybe an igloo or a snowman, but then immediately dismissed the idea as I was, in fact, a grown man, and not a 6-year-old child.

We were soon in Nunburnholme, where I imagined a Mother Superior speeding atop a Yamaha, although we didn't go into the village as such but just skirted past the church. It is here that we met a group of three hikers doing the Wilberforce Way, they told us, and they had also had second thoughts that morning when the rain had quickly turned to snow. They had set off from Pocklington and were heading to Market Weighton, and they asked us about the walking conditions, but they did not look amused when we told them to watch out for the snow. We reckoned they were about halfway along their route, as were we, and after wishing them well, we plodded on.

The church itself was incredibly old, something which might sound obvious, but also something we should give at least a bit of attention. For instance, a part of this church is around 1,000 years old. Think about that. Parts of this building have sat here for around a thousand years.

The part in question is an Anglo-Saxon cross, found during renovations in the late 1800s. It was discovered walled up in the church, possibly put there for safekeeping by some concerned do-gooder centuries ago. When the Victorians discovered it, they put it back together, and it can now be seen inside the church. Unfortunately, although they meant well, when they put it back together, they mounted it back to front. This is a great reminder that if you don't really know what you are doing, don't get involved, which is actually quite a good tip in life in general when you think about it. I find that this rule comes in really handy for getting out of stuff practically all the time, in fact.

Just after the church, a sign pointed north, though it was covered in snow which had stuck to its side. A quick rub with a gloved hand told us that this was indeed our path, and we followed a hedge along the side of a field towards a wood on the side of a hill.

Almost immediately, an exceptionally old lady walking her equally old dog could be seen coming towards us. She looked like she was dressed for arctic exploration, with thick leather boots, some kind of dead animal coat with what looked like a dead fox wrapped around her head. Her yappy little dog was wearing a tartan coat and a vicious smile, with sharp teeth protruding from his lower lip.

She eyed us up and down, and immediately told us that we were not dressed appropriately for the cold weather, and then asked us how far we were going. I was just about to answer when she carried on, telling us that wherever we are going, we probably won't make it and that we should probably prepare to die in a ditch within the next mile or two.

If you have ever had one of those conversations with someone that is completely one way, then you will know exactly what I mean when I talk of this encounter. I'm not sure she would have even listened had we managed to get a word in edgeways, but it didn't matter as we couldn't anyway.

Once she had said her speel, she wandered off muttering something under her breath that was unintelligible, so I had great satisfaction in saying *I curse you, and hope that something slightly unpleasant happens to you, like an onion falling on your head,* confident that she couldn't hear me and wasn't listening anyway. She turned around, looked me in the eye, and said *how rude,* before stomping off for good, with me mumbling *sorry,* which of course she certainly didn't hear.

I do have a habit of saying silly things sometimes, which is probably a result of never having grown up properly, you see. And sometimes I deal with rude people in perhaps not the best way, for which my wife tells me off severely and which is a lesson I really should learn, but clearly have not yet done so.

It seemed like the animals had loved the fact that it had snowed, as in the next field we saw a couple of hares followed by a fox, although the latter didn't seem interested in the former, while overhead a barn owl circled, observing us all

A WALK ON THE WILD SIDE

attentively. A short section of slippery road, again apparently unused today, then led us onto a track which took us up a gentle hill into the woods. Unfortunately, gentle soon gave way to tiring, and although we were all out of breath down to a man, it certainly helped to keep us warm.

The snow once again became deeper, to the point that it was challenging to keep to the path, and had it not been for the farm ahead of us which we directly aimed for, as well as our incredible navigational skills, we would probably have walked right across a farmer's field. This was Wold Farm, and a young man had been watching us approach as he was messing with a small tractor. When we got closer, he asked us why we had walked across his field and not used the path.

Arriving at the main road, we took a moment to enjoy the panoramic views to the west, and I, for one, didn't realise we had climbed so high. As we took in the magnificent sight, it started to snow again, so we trundled on.

It must have been the geography, as we hadn't really changed direction, but for some reason, the wind was now blowing the snow straight into our faces. I could hear Rob and Chris cursing, so I joined in just for the fun of it as I pulled my hood around my head. This did not really have any useful effect, in fact, it focused the pain on the centre of my face alone, and each snowflake stung my skin as it impacted, as it was no longer soft snow but was basically almost ice. This would not have been so bad had it just been one or two flakes, but the wind had now picked up, and we were effectively walking straight into a blizzard.

The visibility closed in, and it suddenly dawned on me that this was a long 9 miles, and I suspected once again a certain amount of creativity regarding the day's mileage. I said nothing though, as I just wanted to keep my head down and plod on and to get this day over with.

We edged along the side of the hill, which was shallow and rose gently to our right, all the while keeping our heads firmly down. A small wood offered at least some respite, but only for a minute, and when we emerged back out into the open, I had the impression that I was being sandblasted once again.

There was nothing to do other than to keep putting one foot in front of the other, and at this point, although my feet were still dry, they were absolutely freezing. I had my hands in my pockets, too, which did not seem to make any difference either, and my fingertips were also feeling the strain of the cold. I don't usually walk with my hands in my pockets; in fact, I tell my kids off for doing so. *What happens if you fall with your hands in your pockets* I ask them. *You will scrape your face off and then have no face* is usually what I say next.

I'm not sure how long it took before we got

to the road, but I know that when we did so, it gave us all a small boost as we knew that our final destination was almost in sight. As a double bonus, the path led us into a somewhat sheltered valley and turned to the west, which gave us at least some protection from the biting winds.

Coming to a junction, we stopped to get our bearings and realised we were near Kilnwick Percy. I had been there a while back, on a hot summer's day, and had enjoyed a peaceful stroll around the grounds of what is now a Buddhist meditation centre. Unfortunately, I had my kids with me, and as kids tend to do, they ran around a bit enjoying the open air and the good weather. I wouldn't mention this, but one of the teachers of my youngest son Max had also decided to visit the centre that same day, presumably with a bit of meditation in mind, which completely went out of the window when he saw her and ran over to see her, thrilled as any child is to bump into their teacher when out in the wild. Her face was a picture, but she was very polite, and after a quick hello, I excused us all, and we moved on.

The sheltered valley did not last long, and as the path turned abruptly to the right and led up a hill, we found ourselves walking straight into a blizzard once again. Every footstep became an intense effort, and we seemed to be making little progress in the ever-deepening snow. Halfway up this hill, however, we found ourselves walking along the edge of a wood, and the difference was vast, as the trees sheltered us from the bulk of the wind and the snow. For the first time in a while, we were able to have a conversation, and the question on everyone's lips was *are we there yet*.

Thankfully, the answer was yes, almost, and we figured we had just over a mile left, though at the pace we were going this was going to take us longer than it usually would. We were all shattered and struggling to make our way through the thick snowdrifts, and could not wait to get to Millington.

We finally caught sight of the village, which was far below us in the valley, and as we edged along the top of Whinny Hill, our thoughts turned to how we were going to get down this steep slope. Chris said he was just going to chuck himself down the hill, and I am not sure if he meant that he was going to slide down it or just run. Robin was a bit more cautious; he was the first aider after all, and I was somewhere in between.

As it was, we passed through the gate that led through to the steep path down into Millington and decided to try to sledge down the hill. I figured this would be fairly safe, as without having an actual sledge I reasoned that there would be a certain amount of resistance that would stop us from, well, dying.

We decided to make it interesting, and turned it into a race, lining up three abreast just beyond the gate. There was no one else either coming up or going down, so we had a free run at it, and as Robin did the countdown that ultimately led to go, I could feel my heart racing.

Upon the signal, I slid off, and . . . nothing. I figured the snow was a bit too thick and glanced across at the others. Chris had not moved either, though Robin had moved around 6 feet before becoming stuck himself.

We all figured out at the same time that we were going to have to find another way down the hill, at which point Chris jumped up and started running, as after all the race was still on. Robin did the same, and I was the last to go and was initially at the back. Chris had started out in the lead, but with shorter legs, this did not last long, as Robin soon overtook him.

I was firmly at the back and appeared to have no chance of catching up, and as we all thundered down the hill, we must have made something of a sight had anyone been around to watch, which of course there wasn't.

At some point, Chris tripped and went down, and with Robin just a short distance behind, the inevitable happened, and he went down too.

I shouted *losers* as I passed the both of them, and enjoyed my lead for a good five seconds. I was glancing back to see what they were doing, and this is perhaps not the best thing to do when you are running as fast as you can down a steep hill.

Obviously, I was the next to go down, and I remember tumbling in the snow, going completely over at least twice.

Robin and Chris were now back up and running, but not for long, as Chris went down again almost immediately, but this time he must have been on compacted snow, and slid surprisingly quickly and was soon well ahead of us all.

Robin decided to do the same, as the path at this point of the hill had been well used, probably by children sledging earlier in the day. When I say children, I mean proper children and not big kids like us.

I joined in but found that I was not as slippery as the other two, so got back on my feet again, but only managed a dozen or so yards before I fell and did a few cartwheels before coming to a halt in another snowdrift.

I got up and realised that I was covered head to toe in snow, as were the other two, and resigned myself to defeat, as both were some way ahead of me at this point. I did not give up though and gingerly jumped down the hill, taking giant strides in what seemed a somewhat futile attempt to catch the others up.

For a while, all was well, with Rob and Chris sliding steadily down the hill, and me running through the snow, raising my knees as high as I could with each step, which must have made me look absolutely stupid if I say so myself.

I then had an idea, and quickly stopped and took out the waterproof cover for my rucksack, opened it out and sat on it, intending to use it as a sledge. Nothing happened at first, but when I pulled it tight and gave myself a push, I started to move.

I was soon flying down the hill, although some way behind the others who were still going at a good pace, but I thought I could sense that I was slowly catching up, though this was barely discernible.

For what seemed like an eternity, but was probably just a few seconds, we all flew down the hill, with Chris and Rob neck and neck at the front, and me trailing somewhere behind.

It was at this point that I reckon Rob and Chris realised that they were heading for a fence, something which I probably figured out a few seconds later, but we were all beyond the point at which we could have stopped ourselves anyway.

Instead, Rob and Chris chose to crash themselves, apparently into each other, and just as they ground to a halt, giggling relentlessly, I hit them both from behind.

We all sat there motionless in the snow for a minute and then burst out laughing, dragging ourselves up and congratulating each other for still being alive and for not having broken our necks. I counted my fingers and figured that I had lost none on the way down, although my back was aching a little bit. There was a bit of a disagreement over who had won between Chris and Robin, and they asked me to adjudicate, so I did the only thing I could and declared myself the winner.

As we walked off to the village, which was now clearly visible a short distance away, Rob had developed a limp and Chris had apparently been inhaling some sort of laughing gas, unable as he was to stop giggling.

The village appeared as a winter wonderland. It was now starting to get dark, and the streetlights had begun to come on, and the snow glowed magically beneath them. We made our way to the village hall, where we thankfully found the lights on and the door open, along with a note telling us to make ourselves at home and that the warden would be along later to check on us.

The heating was on too, which was welcome, and we immediately decided to get out of our cold, wet clothes and to put the kettle on. We found the camp beds, got them set up, and then took turns to have a shower to both clean up and warm up.

This village hall was surprisingly suitable for a night on the trail, and before this, I didn't even know you could stay in places such as this. Rob had found out about it after a friend had told him about his stay here a while back, and all in all, the decision to stay here was definitely a good one.

Once we were all cleaned up and had

changed into dry clothes, our attention turned to food. The breakfast was included in our stay, but the evening meal wasn't. This was not a problem, however, as there was a pub of very fine repute in the village, so after a second cup of tea, we ventured back out into the wilds and headed straight to the Gait Inn.

There was no phone signal in the village, and on the way to the pub, our attempts to ring our other halves proved unsuccessful, until that is, we stumbled across a manhole cover in the road. As I moved around, pointing my phone this way and that, I suddenly noticed my phone briefly got 5 bars of signal. I moved around again, and when I was back on the manhole cover, it flew back up. Calling the others over, who were variously standing on tables and climbing up the sides of peoples' houses, their phones too offered a better signal on the manhole cover. So, it was there that we stood to make our respective phone calls, which must have been an odd sight, all crammed together in the middle of the road. If a car came along now, whoever was driving it would get three for the price of one.

The pub proved to be your typical cosy country pub, with a roaring fire that we were thankfully sat right next to. Robin got us a drink while we perused the menu, with me deciding on meat pie, Robin going for steak and Chris choosing lasagne.

We chatted about the days walk and figured we had done around 12 miles rather than the expected 9, an anomaly which we squarely blamed on Robin. This distance had also taken us a considerably longer time than it normally would due to the snow. The weather forecast showed much of the same for tomorrow, but we were determined to carry on, although we all agreed to revisit this decision in the morning, depending on what we would see when we opened the curtains the following day.

The food was lovely, and we all had a dessert as our appetites were somewhat ravenous due to the effort we had put in that day, and I particularly enjoyed my spotted dick.

As we left the pub, we all congregated on the manhole cover to once again ring our other halves, who did not seem to appreciate our merry phone calls for some unknown reason, which is when we realised that we had perhaps stayed in the pub for a bit longer than we had initially intended to.

MILLINGTON TO THIXENDALE

We woke nice and early, and it was still pitch-black outside. The glow of the old-fashioned sodium streetlights, however, illuminated a snow-covered scene outside which looked incredibly beautiful, although it was probably freezing out there as it was pretty cold in here.

We soon had breakfast on the go, which included all the usual elements of a full English, and as there were only three of us, there was more than enough to go around. With the extra food we had, we made some sandwiches to take with us for lunch as we did not expect to pass any shops today. Finally, we refilled our camel bags with water and were soon ready to go.

The warden had instructed us to simply lock the door and post the keys through the letter-box, which we found ourselves doing, and although it was still technically dark, we could see the first light of dawn in the east, which is good, as that was exactly the direction we were heading. We guessed that the warden had popped by later last night while we had been in the pub, but as it was, we never got to meet him or her to thank them for the stay, which is a shame, as we really enjoyed it.

Our first obstacle would be figuring out how to get to the top of Whinny Hill, which we had so unceremoniously fallen down the previous evening. After wandering through the deserted village, as anyone with even an ounce of sense was still in bed, and with fresh snow resting on every available surface of each and every house, we soon passed a frozen pond and found ourselves looking straight up the hill.

All signs of our unorganized descent were gone, and there were no other footprints, suggesting we were the first idiots to try to get up this hill today. There was only one way to tackle it, we figured, and after a quick chat, we decided Rob was on point, as he was the biggest, and we duly sent him up the hill to make a path for us lesser mortals.

I was literally walking in the footsteps of a giant when I went second, and behind me, last but certainly not least, was Chris, hopping from one hole to another like an arctic fox.

Once again, it is fair to say that we were all wearing every single item of clothing that we had brought with us, and although I did not know the actual temperature, it was certainly below zero. Every footstep seemed to break through a crust of ice before descending through a foot or so of soft snow, which made the going pretty tough, but this had the effect of getting us warmed up pretty quickly, which is exactly what we needed.

The sky above us was a lot less threatening today, and by the time we got to the top of the hill, which took almost half an hour, we could even see traces of blue sky interspersed with the cloud. We had no choice but to stop to get our breath back at the top as this early morning climb had really taken it out of us, but after a few minutes of doing so, we were ready to go again.

The route today would take us north towards Sylvan Dale, and then around the rather exposed Cobdale, where we would be sharing the path with both the Minster Way and the Chalkland Way, so would likely bump into some other walkers at some point. After this stretch of walking on relatively exposed high ground, we would then descend into a series of valleys for a while, which should give us some protection from the bitterly cold winds, before a series of ups and downs would take us towards Huggate. We would then turn north heading for Fridaythorpe, again following a series of ups and downs, before finally heading towards and finishing at Thixendale where, by the looks of it, we might have to dig the car out of the snow if it was anything like where we were now.

We reckoned this was around 12 miles, but Robin had given us that mileage, so I thought it prudent to have 15 in my head, just in case.

The path at the top of the hill was still covered in snow, but it was much less deep than we had just experienced coming up it, and I presumed that the wind was responsible for this. Luckily, the wind at the minute was not very strong and was sort of coming from behind us, so was probably blowing much of the snow down into the valley to our left.

The sky continued to brighten, which was a good sign and was a complete contrast to the whiteout of yesterday. We were able to walk and talk and enjoy the view, which all around could have been encapsulated in one word – crispy.

The general direction of travel today was definitely north, but it would also involve a multitude of twists and turns and ups and downs. The first of these we found at Sylvan Dale, a small but deep valley that necessitated a winding diversion if we wanted to avoid a harsh climb up a steep and very slippery hill. It was here that we first had to face east, the direction from which the wind came, and the contrast was striking. It was like putting your head into a freezer with a powerful fan blowing chilled air straight into your face, so I put my head down and just got it over with. Chris followed me up the winding path, whereas Robin decided to tackle the hill head-on, and just went for it. We all arrived at the top at more or less the same time, and I must say that this is not because Chris and I wanted to beat Robin to the top, which as Robin pointed out, is exactly what losers would say, wouldn't they?

Sylvan Dale is where the Wolds Way crosses an old Roman road, which is heading northwest towards Garrowby, and south-east towards Warter. Indeed, in the 1800s, Roman ruins were found here that included the foundations of a temple, as well as tiles, coins, and the usual pottery, and some people claim that Millington is the site of Delgovicia, an important Roman town in what was then Britannia, which is one of the most important Roman settlements that have yet to be found. I could literally be walking on a fortune, I thought to myself, but when I looked down, all I saw was sheep poo.

This climb, however, had the effect of warming us up once again, apart from our faces of course, and after this we continued heading north, edging along the top of a hill that looked to offer fine skiing and leg-breaking opportunities to our left. I had not seen the British countryside quite like this for some years and reckoned the last time had probably been around 2010 when the UK enjoyed one of the coldest winters we had had for quite some time. I use the term *enjoyed* loosely, though, as most people find it is quite hard to enjoy your nose freezing and falling off, as I remember almost happening way back then when I couldn't get my car off the drive and had to walk to work for a week.

What we could enjoy at the moment, however, was the small hedge to our right which acted as a windbreak, and protected us from the worst of the winds which were trying to turn us into human ice lollies, of the kind often dug up from the frozen tundra of Siberia after being frozen for thousands of years. We were more than happy when the hedge turned into a small forest, but unfortunately, this luxury was short-lived, and we soon found ourselves edging around it and heading once again straight into the bitterly cold easterly winds.

Following along the top of the valley, a car sat down below us apparently abandoned and had yellow tape stuck variously around it suggesting that the police knew it was there. Unusually for a car, it was on its roof, and its black wheels protruded rudely into the sky. Strangely, this stretch of road was relatively straight, and I wondered what chain of events had led to this odd outcome, though my mind soon wandered back to the cold winds blasting my face.

I came up with a cunning plan that might help me keep warmer, and increased my pace so that I was soon more or less straight behind Robin.

I figured that if I was behind him, I might be protected from the worst of the wind, but in practice, I noticed no difference, although I reckon that I did manage to make him feel quite uncomfortable.

Chris was way ahead of us by now, though we could still clearly see the bright orange of his waterproof cover on his rucksack, at least until he disappeared around the brow of the hill we were edging along. I put my head back down, and just concentrated on taking one step at a time, usually in pre-made holes left by my predecessors, and for much of the next mile, my mind simply went blank.

I came out of my trance-like state when our path suddenly met with a road, and not just any road, but one that had evidently seen traffic and had even been cleared with a snowplough. Unfortunately for us though, this lasted for all of 60 seconds, before we once again walked through a gate into yet another snowy wasteland.

My feet had started to feel really cold, despite wearing two pairs of socks and even though we had been walking for over an hour. We were back in deep snow, which seemed to have gathered in drifts on this section of the path up against a hedge, so we moved out a little into the field where it was not quite so deep. I wouldn't normally do this, as obviously down there somewhere there would usually be crops, but at this time of year and under a foot of snow, this did not seem to be a problem.

Coming the other way, we saw the first person that we had seen that day along with her dog, en excitable black and white sheepdog that was darting around the field in some kind of frenzy. When it saw us, it shot towards us and ran around us a couple of times barking as it did so. It was certainly excited at seeing some frozen snacks wandering towards it, though I am not sure it knew what to make of us exactly, dressed up as we were like Ernest Shackleton or Captain Scott.

The owner was shouting its name and trying to call it back, which was all to no avail, but when she pulled out a dog whistle, it shot straight back to her. I had thought she was shouting a rather rude word, but it turns out the dog is called Banker.

I was also quite surprised that I could hear the dog whistle, as I always assumed that they are inaudible to us mere humans, but hear it I certainly could. With the dog firmly on a lead, and as we drew nearer to her, she introduced herself as Peggy from the village, though which village I am not quite sure, and then she asked us if we were stupid.

Okay, she never actually said that, but she meant it, and commented on how surprised she was to see people out walking today. I was almost ready to point out that she, too, was out walking today, but Chris beat me to it, although in a much more diplomatic way than what I would probably have managed, as he asked her how far she was walking today. Ten miles, she said, and the dog twenty presumably, judging by the way we had just seen it flying around the field.

When we told her we were heading for Thixendale, she told us that the road was closed due to the weather, which again brought images of a snow-covered car waiting for us, and she advised us to go to Wetwang instead, as the road had been cleared there. We explained that this was impossible as we had left a car in Thixendale, to which she simply laughed and wished us luck, adding as she walked away that we would need it, and that if she read of three frozen bodies being found anywhere nearby, she would inform our next of kin for us.

Shortly after this, the path once again turned eastwards, so we hunkered down, drawing our hats and hoods as tightly as we could around our heads, and plodded on. At some point, we crossed a road but did not notice until a while later, when we looked at the map in order to try to find out where the road was. I can only figure that the road was covered in as much snow as the fields, and in our heads-down state, we had simply passed it without noticing. It was a good job that there was no traffic, really.

We followed a track which seemed to be heading towards a farm, Glebe Farm, and presumed we would head through the farmyard, but a signpost directed us down a narrow path which circumvented the farm completely. This was very narrow, and the overgrown hawthorn hedges on either side immediately began to dump copious amounts of snow on us at the slightest touch.

I was in front now, which was not ideal as I was getting the brunt of the barrage, and I might have accidentally grabbed a branch or two as I passed, held it for a couple of seconds and then let it go. I knew my evil plot was successful when I heard a couple of profanities coming from behind me, and was happily revelling in my wicked victory when I took a snowball to the back of my head.

We carried on, and after a short while, the path finished at a road where we should turn left to continue on the Wolds Way; however our plan today involved a brief foray into the village of Huggate, as at the far end of it there was a small pub called the Wolds Inn where we intended to warm up for half an hour and perhaps buy some snowshoes or arrange an airlift. The road through what is supposedly the highest village in the Wolds led us past the church and a kids' park, and a left turn dumped us at the door of the pub, which is a very happy place to be dumped at, especially on a day like today.

Stomping our boots clear of snow, we were surprised to find ourselves in a pub that was already pretty busy with walkers and others, despite only having been open for perhaps an hour or so. We grabbed a table in a cosy corner, and I went off to get us all a drink, and due to the relatively early hour and freezing weather, we had all opted for warm drinks. Rob and I went for a hot chocolate, and Chris went for a warm beer, as he doesn't drink tea or coffee on account of it being bad for you, or so he says.

I was surprised to see a couple of cyclists taking a break in the pub, and we soon got talking to them. I reckoned that cycling on a day such as today, where the roads are basically ice rinks, could be pretty bad for your health, but they told us they were cycling off-road on electric mountain bikes, which actually sounded like quite a bit of fun. These things are all the rage nowadays, and we have bumped into people on them before, and I can personally state that they are capable of what I can only describe as suicidal speeds.

The half-hour went, as all good half hours do, exceptionally quickly, and we were soon bidding farewell to our new found lycra clad friends and their various strange protuberances.

When we went back outside, the snow had all gone, and it was now a balmy 30 degrees Celsius, but then I realised I had taken a wrong turn into the kitchen, so we turned around and went back out into the thick snow.

Huggate is supposed to have one of the deepest wells in England at 116 yards deep, but it is also one of the most well-hidden apparently, and we were thus unable to find it, so we resumed our trek north and re-joined the Wolds Way.

The path led us up a gentle hill, once again and not surprisingly free from traffic, and after we passed a sign that announced Northfield Farm, it became even nicer, tree-lined as it was. After a while, and just before we got to the farm, we turned left and ventured across a cultivated field, with the furrows just about showing beneath the snow, which had all been blown away from here.

At the end of the field, a steep slope led us down into Holm Dale, and we managed to get down this one a bit better than the one at Millington the previous evening as we were no longer behaving like idiots. This downhill, which lasted little more than five minutes, then led to us walking uphill for the next half hour, just to gain the altitude that we had lost, which seemed kind of pointless at the time and made me quite annoyed at nature in general, and this stupid hill in particular.

It was a very nice dry valley, though, and one which was sheltered from the elements to a certain extent. These valleys are thought to be glacial in origin with an almost complete lack of rivers in this area, hence the *dry* reference. I have read that this is because any water quickly soaks through the chalky rock, so rivers are unable to form. A few trees dotted the higher parts of this one too, but other than that, it was otherwise featureless, though it did get steeper as we approached its end.

We climbed to the top and joined a rough track heading into Fridaythorpe, which eventually turned into a proper road as we passed a small farm on our left, where a ramshackle assortment of old 4x4s and tractors were lined up outside, none of which looked remotely roadworthy.

We reached the phone box, and after contemplating but then deciding not to live in it for the rest of the winter, we now had a choice of route. We could either turn left and then immediately right and join a small road strangely called *the road to hell*, though probably not the one referenced by Chris Rea. Alternately, we could go right and walk through the village, which is ultimately what we did, not wishing to risk an encounter with the Prince of Darkness himself, although at least that would probably have been warmer.

We passed a pond and were accosted by some hungry ducks and two geese that had clearly had too much caffeine that morning, and then saw a sign for the church and decided to go and have a look. Another sign warned of dangerous gravestones, whatever that meant, and we carried on carelessly regardless. The church was clearly very ancient, but also well kept, and was most importantly a degree or two warmer inside. I use the term warmer, although it must be said that this is relative, and it was not like we could change into our shorts or anything and sip Bacardis on a deck chair.

After having a good though brief look around, we carried on, and I can happily report that we were not mugged or beaten by any dangerous gravestones. Soon enough, we left the village, which is another one that claims to be the highest in the Wolds, and we embarked on the final leg towards Thixendale.

We were now heading west, and finally had the wind behind us, something which made a huge difference and for which we were very grateful. I wouldn't say I was warm, but for the first time today, I felt as if I was no longer getting colder.

The flatness of the fields soon gave way to yet another valley into which we had to slide down a steep slope once again, this time on our bums, and at the bottom, I was surprised to find a few dozen sheep huddled together. I had imagined that most sheep at this time of year would either be snugly stored away in a barn somewhere or else in somebody's oven, in either case somewhere warmer than this freezing valley. To be honest, they didn't seem that bothered by the cold and were probably coping with it somewhat better than the three of us.

I remembered the last time I had walked down this exact valley I had also been with Robin and Chris, but in addition, had been accompanied by Andy and Rob too, and it had been at the height of summer. I remember this because as Chris had taken a photo of me, I had pulled my pants down and pulled a moonie, and I remember how my wife had not been impressed with my childishness.

There was no chance of that today though, as such actions would probably lead to a rapid temperature drop followed by bits falling off, so we blundered on and up the other side of the valley, still heading west, with passports at the ready as this is where we left our beloved East Yorkshire and entered the badlands of North Yorkshire and all that it entailed. This was perhaps the bleakest place we had encountered on what was certainly becoming some kind of walk on the wild side and was in fact much wilder than anything we had anticipated.

It was an incredibly long and hard slog up the other side of this hill, where the snow had once again accumulated, though we eventually came out at the side of a farm, where we found a road. A quick look at the map suggested that Thixendale, our day's destination, could be reached much quicker if we followed this road to the north, but reasoned that the next leg would only be longer as a result, as we would have to move our starting point accordingly, so we crossed the road and carried on along the actual path.

A narrow track took us between two snow-covered fields, at the end of which we were surprised by the sudden appearance of yet another dry valley. This one was better than the rest, however, as it was Thixen Dale itself, and therefore our last dale of the day, even though our actual finishing point was the village going by the same name, minus the space, a couple of miles further on.

We edged slowly down the steep slope at an angle, along what may have been a track beneath the snow, and despite the covering, we could still make out the vortex that is *Waves and Time*, one of many works of art placed along the length of this walk a few years back. This modern earthwork mirrors the many ancient ones dotting this landscape, and will hopefully be here for a long time to come.

We turned north and followed the curves of the valley and had the pleasure of sharing the next half hour with a barn owl that swooped ahead of us, possibly looking for any items of lunch that might have been disturbed by our very presence. I had always assumed that they hibernate in winter, but this is not true, and they have to continue hunting year-round and can often struggle to find enough to eat in harsh winters such as this one, so they probably appreciate clumsy, smelly hikers that can flush out food and therefore do their work for them.

All too soon, though, the owl was gone, and we were back on tarmac and heading towards the village itself, although the tarmac was purely

A WALK ON THE WILD SIDE

hypothetical being hidden as it was by a layer of snow and ice.

Alarmingly, this is when a car came around the bend at considerable speed, and I figured that the driver did not expect to see walkers on his journey today judging by the speed he was going. Almost as soon as he braked, his wheels locked but his car did not slow down one bit. This was alarming, as there was nowhere for us to go unless we wanted to wrestle with some barbed wire, so instead, we turned around and hurriedly moved the other way back to the gate we had just come through.

We just managed to get out of the way when the car glided past on the sheet of ice that was the road, almost silently, with the driver clearly gesturing some sort of apology as he sauntered by.

In fairness, although we had a quick grumble amongst ourselves about his apparent recklessness in going at speed around a corner, he was not, in fact, going very fast as he passed us, and the chances of any impact had probably been very low, with our collective rotundity very likely damaging any car more than it would damage us when we leaned into the bonnet or the windscreen at such low speeds.

We continued to watch the car slide down the road, which had now changed from going downhill to going uphill luckily for the driver, and we half expected the vehicle to leave the road at any moment. Somewhat miraculously, this never happened, although the car never quite managed to stop either. With its brake lights still on, our last glimpse of the vehicle was as it disappeared around the next bend and disappeared out of sight. We never heard a crash or any other sound indicating that it had gone into a ditch or a field, and there was certainly no explosion that would have been certain in any movie, so with that, we carried on ourselves, although we were certainly a bit warier of the bend up ahead of us. Incidentally, just a few yards around that bend is the Robert Fuller Gallery, well worth a visit in order to have a look at some of his incredibly beautiful paintings, and if you are feeling a bit flush, you might even want to buy one.

Luckily, there proved to be no more traffic between us and the village, which is not surprising given the day's weather, and soon enough, we were at the end of this rather long dale and were walking into the village itself.

We found the car outside the award-winning Cross Keys public house, which was not surprising as that was exactly where we had left it, but what was perhaps surprising was that we did not need to dig it out after all. In fact, the sun had been shining for much of the day here which meant that there was hardly any snow on the car at all, so we wasted no time in dumping our gear in the boot, jumping inside, and heading home, with only one stop at Goodmanham to pick the other car up.

We did find time to pop in the pub, however, as you know how we like to support these local businesses, where a hot chocolate warmed our cockles considerably. We had the place more or less to ourselves and chatted to the barman about how busy the place was at the moment, which was not very, given the weather, but with the clock ticking away and the weather possibly taking a turn for the worse after darkness, we did not hang around.

Only when we got in the car did we realise how cold it actually was out there, and it was absolute bliss when the heating kicked in and finally started to warm the cab up. I had claimed shotgun and huddled around the warm air vent, and Chris was in the back sprawled right across the seat absolutely exhausted. Although we had all greatly enjoyed the last couple of days, we did nonetheless unanimously decide that it would probably be sensible to wait until the weather got at least a bit better before finishing this walk, so in that spirit, we went home for a well-earned rest.

THIXENDALE TO WINTRINGHAM

Almost three weeks had passed since we had walked any of the Wolds Way, and this was primarily because the weather had taken a turn for the worse which would have made it dangerous. The snow that had started to fall as we walked from Market Weighton had actually continued on and off for several days and temperatures had dropped to as low as -15 degrees Celsius. The whole thing had been given a name – The Beast from the East, and had caused much disruption across the entire country.

This weather event had actually contributed to the deaths of many people across the country, including tragically a young girl from Cornwall and a homeless man who was found frozen to death in his tent, among many others, with several more being the victims of road accidents.

Although it was still cold outside, and there was snow on the hills, things had gotten back to normal enough for us to consider finishing the walk without putting anyone at risk. I know that I often portray us as a bunch of inept blokes, and I can assure you that we most certainly are, but when it comes down to it, we are pretty sensible, and would not want to put anyone at risk because we had gone out in adverse weather or without the correct clothing or equipment. This is why we had decided to err on the side of caution and to sit it out, but today I could announce that we were firmly back on the trail.

We met in Wintringham near a very picturesque row of old whitewashed cottages, where we were going to leave Rob's car under a big old tree, and the three of us, Chris, Rob and myself, then drove back to Thixendale to start the walk from where we had left off, which was outside the Cross Keys public house.

Someone had rudely taken our parking space, so after bouncing that car out of the way and putting ours in the spot, we changed into our gear, and once again we were all going for the full winter kit, with hats, gloves, scarves and gaiters being the order of the day. The walk today would involve more exposed hills interspersed with valleys, and there was a probability, albeit a small one, of some further snow, and we were determined that we would stay warmer this time. Finally, before we move on, we didn't really bounce the car out of the way, of course, as that would have been silly. We simply rammed it.

The walk out of Thixendale was swift and sharp, going vertically up a track that immediately got our hearts racing. The crisp cold air meant that we did not over-heat, however, and I, for one, was still fairly cold when we arrived breathless at the top.

The view down onto the village was idyllic, though, and well worth the climb. Several chimneys puffed coal smelling clouds of smoke skywards, which reminded me of my childhood and visits to my grandparents, which did actually warm me somewhat.

I had studied the maps of this area vigorously over the last few days and noted that there was a lot of land around here that was considered open access, which means that you can essentially roam across it at will, within common sense limits of course. The spot where we now stood was one of those such places and was quite easy to access, but I also noted that there were several areas that seemed to be cut off from any roads, tracks or paths, which kind of defeated the point of open access land, in my eyes anyway.

As we headed north, we joined the route of the Centenary Way, which is yet another long-distance footpath that runs through this area. This was devised in order to celebrate the 100th birthday of Yorkshire County Council, which seems a bit odd if you ask me, but anyway, it runs from York to the Wolds and is probably quite a nice route to follow.

The path led us through a busy farmyard where someone with some kind of forklift was moving hay bales onto the back of a wagon, and for a moment the hustle and bustle and noise broke the silence that we are usually accustomed to on these walks.

We continued up a gentle hill, enjoying the views all around which were pretty good today, but eventually uphill gave way to downhill, which proved to be somewhat challenging given that large parts of the path were still frozen. The path turned into a track, which was at least a little better to walk along, but this section of the walk was incredibly exposed to the elements, and I found myself grateful that the weather was holding up much better today than it had been.

The path twisted and turned, and the landscape turned from farmed arable land to some sort of pasture, all the while remaining as exposed as ever, and from somewhere the smell of fire reached us although there was absolutely no sign of one anywhere.

After around half an hour, we re-joined what I would call a proper road, and I knew it was a proper road because as we walked along, we encountered various squashed animals. A wood off to our left now offered itself as the source of the fire, and every now and then we heard the sound of a gunshot or a bird scarer, though which one it was I had no idea. The sound wasn't regular, and sometimes there were multiple shots one after the other, suggesting someone was hunting something, probably something feathered.

This road led us under many old trees, which I imagined probably formed a canopy in the warmer months, but today the skeletal-like figures offered just scattered shadows. A prompt left turn saw us suddenly entering a village, and a quick look at the map told us we were in Birdsall.

Arriving in the village proper, we found ourselves at a junction where in front of us was a very fine building that was actually the estate office. I'm guessing it was Georgian, judging by the windows, but anyway it was very nice and would make a lovely place to live in if you were perhaps a millionaire.

Just after turning right here, I saw a sign for somewhere called Birdsall House, and through the trees down the drive where this sign pointed, you could just make out a hint of a very big house indeed, so I suggested to Rob and Chris that we have a quick look.

Well, no sooner than we had gone barely a hundred yards down the path, a gamekeeper appeared and asked us if we had an appointment. I say gamekeeper, which is a guess, but he had the

A WALK ON THE WILD SIDE

typical look of one, which consisted of a tweed jacket, one of those hats that Sherlock Holmes wears, along with a bloody big double-barrelled shotgun. I'm not sure how he knew we were there, but anyway, I said no, we did not have an appointment, but we were just being nosey and wanted to have a quick look at the house as we passed.

I think he appreciated my honesty and introduced himself as Simon, and he was, in fact, the gamekeeper, although what I had thought to be a shotgun was in fact just a walking stick. He had driven down on a little golf buggy when he had seen us on his camera, he said, as he just happened to be in his office as we had approached.

He was clearly very proud of the place and parked his buggy up so he could come and talk to us, which I saw as a good sign.

It turns out that the house we could see from the road was just an appetiser, and the main house stood a few hundred yards away, which is where Simon said we could go to have a look at now as he was doing his rounds. I don't think he was doing his rounds, though, I think he just wanted someone to talk to, which is something I find with most people when they are at work. I've been incredibly cheeky over the years, and have just asked apparently random people to show me around all sorts of places, and nine times out of ten they have obliged. One of the most interesting places I managed to get a look at was a water pumping station, which might sound a bit boring but was incredible when you are stood next to a water pump blasting through thousands of litres of water every second, and is actually mildly terrifying.

Anyway, Simon took us to have a look at the main hall, and as a double bonus, there were the ruins of a church next to it, which looked absolutely fantastic. He told us that the oldest parts of the house were around 500 years old, and the two wings on either side were added much later. He also told us that the house is very much a family home nowadays, but that you can also get married here if you wish, which I certainly had no plans to do.

The house is home to the Willoughby family, the head of which is known as Baron Middleton, after the original family home Middleton Hall. Death duties forced that one to be sold, which is how the seat ended up here instead, and there is a long history of the Willoughby family in this area.

While most of them are basically a little boring, there are a couple of them that really manage to stand out from the crowd, though not necessarily in an all sort-of good way.

First off is Hugh Willoughby, born in the early 1500s. He served in various roles in the court of Henry VIII but was a soldier by trade. After finding himself out of favour, he had to look for a new job and petitioned to lead an expedition to the

Arctic. Despite having no experience or skills that might be remotely useful, he did, however, come from a very influential family, which landed him the gig. What could possibly go wrong?

Quite a lot, as it turns out. The grand voyage got off to a bad start in 1553, and it took Hugh and his small armada of three ships over two months just to get across the North Sea as far as Norway. Things then took a turn for the worse, with a storm separating one ship from the other two. To cut a long story short, Hugh was never seen alive again, and we only know what happened from his diaries which were recovered later. The storm left them disoriented, with maps that can politely be described as inaccurate, and with compasses that were unreliable. Willoughby sailed around aimlessly this way and that for a few weeks, before winter ice-locked his ship in for the duration.

The following spring, fishermen found Willoughby, his two ships and all of their crew firmly and permanently dead, and somewhat frozen. Although they were assumed to have either starved or frozen to death, it is possible that they died of carbon monoxide poisoning, after doing an incredible job of making their ship airtight in order to keep out the bitter arctic cold. Unfortunately, when they did this, they blocked the flue of their chimney.

The ships were recovered and kept safe until they could be collected by the English, and finally in 1556, some three years after setting off, crews arrived from England to take the ships back home, but sailed into a storm and sank. All that was left was the diary of Hugh Willoughby, perhaps the most unsuccessful arctic explorer ever.

As if Hugh wasn't bad enough, we then have the unfortunate case of Nesbit Josiah Willoughby, one of Hugh's much later descendants. Born in the late 1700s, Nesbit also served on ships, though this time in the Royal Navy. He distinguished himself at the Battle of Copenhagen and was said to be a fierce fighter, but unfortunately, he was also a bit of a nutter and had something of a problem with authority. He was court-martialled in 1801 for insolence towards a superior officer, and because this was not his first offence, he was thrown out of the navy.

Just a couple of years later, though, when war once again reared its ugly head, Nesbit rejoined the navy as a volunteer and again distinguished himself in battle, this time in the West Indies. Unfortunately, his behaviour once again landed him a court-martial, although he somehow managed to get away with this one and was simply told to please stop swearing at people, and especially at the officers.

By 1810, Nesbit was somehow commanding his own ship, and while there is no question as to his bravery, he was somewhat lacking when it came to tactics. As a result, he suffered a huge defeat to a French ship, despite his own vessel both outgunning and outmanning his foreign foe. Realising that his career in the navy was probably over and done forevermore, he went to work for the Russians but was then captured by the French, and although he managed to escape to England, his reputation and career were now both in tatters, and that was the last we hear from him until he died in 1849.

He is fondly remembered, however, as one of the most reckless characters in British naval history and his obituary reads as follows:

He was eleven times wounded with balls, three times with splinters, and cut in every part of his body with sabres and tomahawks; his face was disfigured by explosions of gunpowder, and he lost an eye and had part of his neck and jaw shot away... and at Leipzig had his right arm shattered by cannon shot.

We might then find it quite surprising to discover that he was knighted twice, and I wondered if this meant that people had to address him as Sir Sir Nesbit Willoughby. Anyway, this distinction led to him being nicknamed twice-knightly, and if any of this sounds like anyone you may know, it is because Nesbit is the inspiration for none other than Hornblower, as played so well by Ioan Gruffud in the TV series of the same name.

While all of this was fascinating, it was time to move on, and we told Simon that we really should be going. He asked us where we were heading, and when we told him we were walking the Wolds Way, he told us we were not. His bluntness stunned us, and I wondered if he was going to finish us off there and then and bury us in the woods, and had simply lured us so far into the grounds to do so, but then he told us that that the Centenary Way went through Birdsall, but the Wolds Way most definitely did not, and that we had clearly taken a wrong turn.

I could feel eyes burning into me, as it was me that had the map at the moment and could do no better than suggesting that we head back the way we had come in order to get on the right path, and how this little diversion had all been worth it after having seen the hall, but no one was buying any of it.

Around 40 minutes later, we arrived at a signpost that quite clearly pointed left for the Centenary Way and right for the Wolds Way, and wondered how on earth we had all missed it, and I may have wondered this aloud just to remind Robin and Chris of their complicity in my error, as they had not seen it either. We had probably spent over two hours going to Birdsall and back, and while it had been very nice, we now had some serious time to make up, though at least we were now going in the right direction.

This was Deep Dale, and it certainly lived up to its name. We were walking along the top of the valley, and almost mirroring us on the other side were a group of cows who were following one another in an almost perfect line. Incredibly, though, the cows were halfway up the side of the valley on the extremely steep slope that led up the other side, though I imagined they knew what they were doing.

For the first time today, we began to encounter several other small groups of walkers. They were coming from Wharram Percy, which was just up ahead of us, and a number of them stopped to have a quick chat.

Amazingly, one of the people who stopped to talk to us lived just a street away from Robin, which we discovered after going through all the usual conversations that walkers tend to have such as *where are you from, oh I'm from there, whereabouts exactly*, that sort of thing.

We declined to mention that we had wasted a good couple of hours after missing a rather obvious signpost pointing us in the right direction, and after a few minutes we thought it best to move on.

A sheep track took us down to the valley floor and into Wharram Percy, which is on the list of my top ten favourite places and is incidentally in the distinguished company of such delights as Malham and Kielder. We passed a small pond where a dog was trying its best to drown itself while trying to drag out of the water a branch which was as big as half a tree, and we went to sit down on a bench near the ruined church. The owner was trying to get the dog to come out of the water, but Fido was having none of it, and the incident provided a humorous minute or two for us three as well as some other people who had stopped what they were doing to witness this exciting event.

I did have some sympathy because one of my dogs goes ballistic at the sight of water, and in fact, I think she must be half camel as she can seem to smell it from miles away. I brought her here once, and although I managed to keep her out of the pond, she did manage to slip the lead a little further on, and I last saw her running down a crystal clear and thankfully shallow chalk stream after which she vanished for half an hour, causing me considerable worry. When she eventually came back, she had changed colour and had some roadkill in her mouth, which she faithfully spat at my feet as some kind of bribe, I imagine.

Anyway, Wharram Percy, which is an excellent name in and of itself, is a place of great interest to archaeologists for a whole variety of reasons. It is, according to English Heritage, one of the biggest and best-preserved of Britain's deserted medieval villages, of which there are a staggering 3,000 or thereabouts, and of which there are countless around here, with this one being abandoned around the year 1500.

The earliest settlement here dates from just

over 2,000 years ago, though the village itself probably sprung up around 1,000 years ago. It was certainly thriving by the time of the Domesday Book, which even names the chief landowners as Lagmann, Carli, and the suspiciously Viking sounding Ketilbjorn.

Unfortunately for them, however, William the Conqueror did what he did best, and confiscated their lands, and passed them on to one of his mates. This is how the Percy family first came to own land in the area, which also helps explain the name, and from then on, their influence only grew. Village life was, however, somewhat decimated by the plague sometime in the mid-1300s.

As the rising price of wool induced many landowners to turn arable land into pasture, the peasants found that they were forced off the land as a result, which helped further depopulate many medieval villages such as Wharram Percy. Although nobody knows exactly when the village lost its last villager, thereby becoming, well, not a village anymore, the disappearance of the very last farmstead soon after 1636 is taken as concrete proof that the place was now well and truly empty, although it had probably been so for quite some time before this.

The village then literally disappeared into history, with most traces of it simply vanishing and leaving not much more than the church and some earthworks where other buildings had once stood, but in the 1950s, when the archaeologists arrived, the place came back to life, at least every summer, and the excavations went on well into the 1990s. As a result, this is now one of those places in the world that gets archaeologists and historians excited, which quite frankly sounds like an oxymoron if I am truly honest.

They learnt a lot by digging the place up, and some of what they discovered is actually quite interesting. For instance, some of the human remains unearthed here suggest that our medieval ancestors believed in zombies, yes, I said zombies, so when burying the dead, they would sometimes chop them up, perhaps decapitating them just to be on the safe side, and even burning whatever was left of Uncle Bob and Aunt Fanny just to be really, really sure. Sometimes this would be done well after death, and the body would have to be dug up first, which would presumably have been really creepy. Anyway, the idea was to stop revenants, which is apparently the proper name for animated corpses, from rising from their graves. Once risen, you see, they would get up to all sorts of mischief if left unchecked, such as spreading diseases and mugging passers-by, as if rising from the grave wasn't enough in itself. There, I told you some of it was quite interesting.

Anyway, those clever archaeologists learned all this when they found various marks on the bones of ten individuals they exhumed from here and were able to discount suggestions of cannibalism or possibly that the people had been mistreated after death because they were strangers, which means that the fear of zombies theory is the most likely of them all.

Looking at the ruins of the church today, which is called St Martin's by the way, with its roof long gone and its tower half-collapsed, you get the impression that it has stood like this for centuries. However, this is not so. Photos exist of the church from as recently as the 1950s, which is of course when the archaeologists first arrived in any great numbers, that show the church complete with roof and fully functional tower, and quite splendid it looked too. In fact, the church remained in general use for hundreds of years after the abandonment of the village. Some alterations were made to the church as late as 1917, and while the last burial here was way back in 1906, the last wedding was in 1928, and the last service in the church was as late as 1949. The tower partially collapsed in the winter of 1959, and the roof was removed after this, leaving what we have today, which has since been made stable for the time being at least.

I wandered into the church and had a look around, and it is clear that some work has been done to try to at least stop the decay, but the fact that it is open to the elements certainly doesn't help, although it should last quite a few years yet as a ruin anyway.

It was time to move on, and we wandered past the church and through a gate that probably served to keep sheep out of the site, as just at the other side there were perhaps fifty of them, all stood around making a torrential noise and an equally torrential mess.

There were some cottages here too, which were clearly not lived in but would certainly make a wonderful home for someone who wanted to live in the back of beyond without electricity, gas, or presumably running water while witnessing a cavalcade of visitors every bank holiday Monday.

The track led us up a hill, and there were a couple of information boards that told you a bit more about the village, but sadly they failed to mention zombies which was clearly the best bit.

Uphill turned to downhill, and after going through a large gate, we crossed the small stream where my dog had previously gone AWOL, and the memory of it made me smile. She knew she was in trouble when she came back, and I can clearly see in my mind her big sad eyes when I rebuffed the meaty gift that she had so carefully delivered to me in person.

This is also where we crossed the disused railway line, which at one point led both north and south from here, although today you could only really follow it to the north. If you try to follow it to the south, you will really hurt yourself when you walk into the bricked-up northern end of

Burdale Tunnel, which at just short of a mile long is now home to several hundred bats. Although you can't see it from here, I promise you it is there but is more or less impossible to see through the dense trees, even in winter.

This railway line was once part of a grand plan to link Newcastle up with Hull, but it quickly ran into financial difficulties, partly because of the tunnel.

When the builders had first started work on the tunnel, they had anticipated that they would be digging through relatively stable and somewhat dry chalk but had soon encountered pretty wet and unstable clay. In order to save money, they changed the design of the tunnel from twin-track to single-track, but this was not enough, and eventually, the company had to ask George Hudson, the not so squeaky-clean businessman we last encountered at Londesborough, for some money. Unfortunately, he was by then going through what can only be described as a difficult patch himself, and he of course later had to flee the country.

Eventually, however, they managed to finish the line regardless, and services began in 1853 with the satisfyingly named train service being dubbed the *Malton Dodger*. It enjoyed varied success, but was never what you would call profitable, and was actually at its busiest during the Second World War when it was used to ferry troops and ammunition to the many airfields of East Yorkshire. It finally closed for good in 1958 and has since then started to be gradually absorbed back into the landscape, with many aspects of the line now completely gone, including several substantial buildings, and the tunnel is perhaps the only component that will be here long after everything else has vanished completely, which will be not too far in the future probably.

I have been in this tunnel once or twice, although now that it has bats in it this is completely forbidden, but anyway, a roof collapse in 1978 and a further one in the mid-1980s makes this both unadvisable and potentially the last thing you might ever do if you did decide to go in, so on we plod instead.

The proper work began now, and the path soon became very steep, hemmed in on either side by overgrown banks of nettles and small bushes even at this time of year.

Soon enough, the path began to flatten out, and we enjoyed glorious views when we momentarily stopped and had a look behind us.

I am reminded of one time when I came up here many years ago, and I was with my wife on our non-honeymoon shortly after we had been married. It was a beautiful sunny day way back then, in stark contrast to the cold we encountered today, and we had been walking up this very hill back to our car, which we had left in the car park at the top.

A WALK ON THE WILD SIDE

We stopped when an older couple came the other way and had a chat about this and that, which actually went on for quite some time. They were a very nice couple, and although I cannot remember what she looked like, he was short, with a flat cap and a nice jacket, spectacles and a big bushy beard. He was interested in my camera, which was an early digital SLR, and was my first what I would call proper digital camera that I have owned and which I still have to this day, and at the end of the conversation, he asked me if I had heard of Bill Bryson. I had, I told him, adding that he was a fine writer and that I had read one or two of his books. Well, to cut a long story short, I have since become convinced that this was Bill Bryson, and he was undercover, so to speak, doing a bit of research. I only came to this conclusion when I much later saw a photo of Bryson, as although I had read some of his work, I had never paid much attention to the thing on top of his neck, which is his face, of course. As further proof, he talked about Wharram Percy in his next book, but he never mentioned the handsome chap with the camera that he had met there.

Coming to the car park, it was surprisingly full, and one or two lunatics were actually sat on folding chairs they had presumably brought along, their car boots open and enjoying some sort of picnic. We said hello to them, and wondered how on earth they managed to sit out here without freezing to death. We were barely keeping warm even though we were walking, and we had noticed earlier that when we had stopped, we had quickly become very cold indeed, so had kept our breaks short as a consequence.

A bit of road walking followed, which was pretty hard on our feet after all these miles, but after a few minutes, we were back on soil which led us along a muddy track across a field and down a slight hill. Halfway across this field, we came across a raven that was enjoying a particularly fine meal of rabbit a la rue, and I noted that he was making industriously effective use of whatever was left of it, and had probably been feasting on this particular delicacy for a few days now, judging by the state of it.

The raven refused to get out of the way as we passed and merely bounced around a little on the track, and when we had passed, he carried on with his dinner as if we had never been there, although I reckon he was keeping at least one beady little eye on us.

We emerged onto a small country lane next to a row of houses which looked as if they had been placed here for absolutely no reason as there was nothing else around here. It turned out though that we were in the village of Wharram-le-Street, but it was surprisingly well spaced out. The rest of the village was a little further up and was where we also found the main road which we turned north on.

The name comes from the fact that a Roman road is once thought to have run nearby, but this was something that was *discovered* in the nineteenth century without much evidence, other than noticing that a lot of the roads around here were, erm, straight.

To be honest, the next village just off to the east is a lot more interesting than where we were currently stood, but it was unfortunately not a part of our itinerary today. That village would be Duggleby, and it has at least two things going for it, with the first one being Duggleby Howe.

Think of Duggleby Howe as the north of England's version of Silbury Hill. At around 120 feet across, it must have taken a heck of a lot of work to build without the use of so much as a single spade, but build it they did. It is believed to date from the late Neolithic era, which means the new stone age to laymen such as myself, and this makes it around 5,000 years old, illustrating once again just how ancient this part of the country is.

It was mainly excavated by a man called John Mortimer, a local man who was born in Fimber and went to school in Fridaythorpe, which of course we passed through earlier, and he was by all accounts quite a responsible archaeologist. At one point, Mortimer worked with someone who was not so much a responsible archaeologist, the Canon William Greenwell, particularly at the excavation of Danes Graves, but more of that later. Lastly, Mortimer had an absolutely ace beard, and he ran a brewery, so I think we would have got along just fine. Sadly, after a lifetime spent studying archaeological depressions in the ground, Mortimer went bankrupt in the financial depression of 1877, when the price of grain fell dramatically, quickly putting him out of business.

The second thing that Duggleby has going for it is that it is the source of the Gypsey Race, which is not any kind of event but is, in fact, a rare chalk stream that is said to only flow when bad things are going to happen, and is thus nicknamed the *woe waters*. It has flowed the year before the great plague, before both the world wars and most recently, before the Coronavirus, so there you go. This seasonal river flows out into the North Sea through Bridlington Harbour, and hopefully takes all of its bad luck with it, and is the most northerly chalk stream on the Wolds, making it the most northerly one in England.

Anyway, it is time to move on. After leaving the village, we headed off-road and uphill, as always, though the gradient was pretty calm and gradual. Crossing another road, we found ourselves now going downhill, which was more than welcome, and I, for one, had now had enough and just wanted to stop walking. Unfortunately, however, the worst was yet to come.

After a relatively calm descent, we now

found ourselves looking down the cliff that formed an area marked on the map as The Peak. It certainly lived up to its name, and as we all scratched our chins and wondered how on earth we were going to get down this slippery grassy slope, Chris just went for it.

He was using his hiking poles to, well, to stop himself dying I reckon, and for a minute he seemed to be managing it. Almost imperceptibly, though, he sped up and was soon running down the hill at a speed to suggest he was starring in Jurassic Park and there was something in his mirror that was closer than it appeared. He was on fire, and would probably have qualified for the Olympics, had he not then tumbled and fallen the last 50 feet.

Robin and I cringed as Chris came to a tumbling stop at the bottom of the hill, shutting our eyes at the worst bit. To add to this, he just lay there, and Robin asked me if we should maybe call an ambulance, but I said no because I had a bivvy bag in my rucksack that would double as a body bag.

We shouted down to him, almost in unison, asking if he was alright, which he must have been because he replied with something that was barely audible, but that clearly started with F and ended in off, but he still didn't move.

Slowly, ever so slowly, the two of us began to make our way down this slippery slope, edging sideways and at an angle relative to the hill. How we did not slip as well is anybody's guess, because the slope was such a combination of steep and wet that it was treacherous, and possibly one of the worst hills we had come down on this walk. I can only ever remember something like this once before, and anyone who has walked Wainwright's Coast to Coast will be more than familiar with the descent from Dent Fell just before Nannycatch Gate, which one of my friends called a widow-maker.

We got to him, he had still not moved at this point, and looked down pityingly on his twisted form. His arms and legs pointed in unnatural directions, but alarmingly he was laughing. He is in shock, I said to Robin, to which he replied that he wasn't and that he's just an idiot. We helped him up, and after counting his fingers and seeing if he could count ours, we declared him medically fit to continue, and pushed him on.

A road, or track, ran along the valley here, which we followed as it twisted through a nearby farm. A vicious dog barked at us, probably signalling that it wanted to remove our intestines, but luckily it was on a thick and heavy chain that made this outcome at least slightly less likely.

I thought we would be walking into a wood next; however, a sign pointed us around it and away from the well-laid track, although just a few minutes later we were back on this track, which

A WALK ON THE WILD SIDE

made the diversion seem slightly pointless.

This wood was noisy with the sound of birds, and seemed to go on for a long way, but must have been very thin as occasionally we caught glimpses of daylight as we looked through it.

A road announced itself before we could see it as various cars whizzed by unseen, but when we got to it, it was devoid of traffic and just sat silently between the trees. Crossing over and passing a Yorkshire Water borehole, which is, by the way, some of the finest water in the world and is a key ingredient of Yorkshire Tea, one of the finest teas in the world, another wood immediately presented itself, with a wide track disappearing off into it in a very straight line.

Also noisy with the sound of birds, this wood had extra wildlife as we saw first a couple of hares, which just ran on the track ahead of us and made no effort to flee into the woods. Next, though, we encountered a single solitary deer, and although we stopped as soon as we saw it and whilst it was still quite far ahead of us, we still managed to spook it, and it was gone in less than a second.

We saw no sign of it as we neared where it had stood, and presumed it long gone, so continued our walk.

Robin and Chris were having one of those pointless arguments about who would win in a fight between Superman and Captain Marvel, and although I am not really into superheroes, it was quite an amusing argument. Rob was claiming that Superman's' superior Kryptonian DNA meant that he would win, as it gave him powers such as flying and super strength. Captain Marvel, on the other hand, was just a badass, so who knows. I'm going to flip a coin and say I agree with Robin on this one, and reckon Superman would win.

Neither Robin nor Chris, however, is aware of the Gin Genie when I ask them. I know I said I am not into superheroes, but my mind is full of all sorts of useless trivia, and the stranger something is, the more likely I am to remember it.

Anyway, Gin Genie, real name Beckah Parker, is actually kind of given away by her title. She has the power of seismokinesis; that is, she is able to generate seismic vibrations, or earthquakes in English. As you may have guessed, and as her name suggests, she can only do this when she has had a tot or two of gin, so if my wife could be a superhero, she would probably want to be this one. Furthermore, her powers, Gin Genie's, not my wife's, were exactly concurrent with her blood alcohol level. You may have noticed that I said *were*. Unfortunately, as is usually the case when you are drunk, accuracy was not her forte, and she often misdirected her powers at her own teammates, and actually managed to kill herself while on a mission due to being somewhat worse for wear, so let that be a lesson to us all.

There are more pointless superheroes out there, too, with just a couple more that really stand out for their lameness. Mr Immortal was just that, and when he discovered he could not die, he decided to put his powers to good use. Doorman has the questionable ability to turn himself into, well, a door obviously. And perhaps the most random? Well, that has got to be Arm Fall Off Boy, I kid you not. Someone actually went to great lengths to create a superhero that purely and simply has the power to detach his arm and beat you to death with it. That alone is why I am not into superheroes, I might add, although at least his action figure would probably have had his actual power, in a roundabout way nonetheless.

With our pointless conversation over, and with me clearly the winner in the pointless stakes, we came out of the wood at the top of a hill that offered such stunning views north towards the Yorkshire Moors that we just had to stop and each take about a hundred photos.

Below us, various villages dotted the landscape though it was hard to know which was which, although the brewery at Knapton stood out like a sore thumb with its industrial might rising above anything else in this otherwise rural landscape.

With our memory cards full, we edged carefully down the steep slopes and went through a gate at the bottom which led us onto a track disappearing off into the distance with no end in sight.

A quick look at the map, however, suggested that we were not far off our finishing point of Wintringham, which gave us a new lease of life on this last stretch of track. It was a more or less featureless walk, with splendid views nonetheless, and we therefore thoroughly enjoyed this bit.

We had the track to ourselves which kind of leads you into a false sense of security, so when a couple of pheasants came flying out of the bushes at head height making a tremendous cackling racket, I think we all nearly had simultaneous heart attacks. I don't know why these creatures do this, as it happens all the time. They wait until you are almost upon them, and then they shoot out. This is probably not to their advantage. Although I meant them no harm whatsoever, if I had been carrying a shotgun, I probably would have used it just out of sheer terror alone.

We followed this track for a mile, where signs pointed left to Thorpe Bassett and right to Wintringham. Although we were not going into Thorpe Bassett today, the land we were crossing right now is part of the Thorpe Bassett Estate, long owned by the Cholmley family.

I have said many times that no matter where you go in England, there is usually a fascinating story to tell, and this place is no exception. And although I do tend to wander off when telling these stories, once again this one will be worth it, I promise.

In the village, there is a war memorial that remembers, among others, George Francis Cholmley. It is his story that is fascinating, and which is part of a much larger story that had a direct impact on the eventual allied victory in the First World War.

George was born in 1892, and enjoyed a privileged upbringing on the family estate, though he chose the Royal Navy as his career. By the start of the war in 1914, Cholmley had been promoted to a Lieutenant-Commander and found himself in charge of one of the navy's newest and most capable submarines.

HMS E3, despite its not very creative name which designated it simply as the third E-class submarine to be built, had a short but interesting life. At the start of the war, she was based in Harwich with Captain Cholmley and his crew of thirty as a key part of the Home Fleet.

On 16 October 1914, E3 set sail into the vast greyness of the North Sea to patrol an area off the island of Borkum, which was the most north-westerly part of Germany. Two days later, and having spotted some enemy destroyers heading out to sea when he arrived in his designated patrol area, Cholmley realised that he could not catch them, but decided to hang around until they returned so as to sink them on their way back to port.

In order to do this, he found a small bay in

which to hide his submarine, which would have been a great plan had the bay not already been occupied by a German U-boat, U27. Apart from the fact that the Germans also showed a bit of a lack of imagination when it came to naming their submarines, this also gives us a clue as to what happened next.

The German U-boat was commanded by Kapitänleutnant Bernd Wegener and was in many ways similar to E3, being only slightly larger and pretty modern for her time, with a similar-sized crew, and had actually been commissioned just three weeks before the E3.

Wegener spotted the E3 immediately and ordered his submarine to dive to battle stations, then spent the next 2 hours slowly and silently lining the British submarine up in his sights.

At around 1330 hours on 18 October, a torpedo fired from U27 hit E3 directly amidships and sank her instantly. Fearing that a second British submarine might be lurking in the shallow waters nearby, Wegener immediately withdrew his submarine but returned half an hour later to look for survivors, though he could find none.

While this is interesting in and of itself, the most important fact to note here is that this was the first time ever that a submarine had been torpedoed and sunk by another submarine, and this event changed the face of warfare for all that followed.

However, the story continues with the U27, which was herself sunk less than a year later, when on 19 August 1915 she was attacked by a Q-Ship called HMS Baralong. Q-ships were basically heavily armed decoy vessels, which hid their weaponry until a U-boat surfaced, which is when the crew would try to send the U-boat straight back down to the bottom again.

This might sound perfectly normal to us nowadays, especially to those who believe the best form of defence is attack, but at the time it was considered unsporting and ungentlemanly, to say the least. At the time, the convention of Prize Rules directed submariners to surface, search and sink merchantmen and freighters only after placing their crews in a place of safety.

Observing these rules, U27 surfaced intending to warn and board the Baralong, but she was fired upon and sunk when she did so. Bernd Wegener and his surviving crew abandoned ship, and some of them managed to swim to another ship in the area, the SS Nicosian.

Quite barbarically, HMS Baralong then machine-gunned the surviving Germans in the water, killing them all, and even executed those that had made it onto the Nicosian. Although this act grossly violated the Hague Convention, the British Government refused to court-martial the officers of HMS Baralong, as they had actually been acting under secret orders and had explicitly been told not to take any prisoners, presumably to keep their activities and existence secret.

As well as a major diplomatic incident, this caused a series of events to follow that would eventually result in an allied victory, as previously mentioned, and it has to be questioned whether this was a deliberate intention of the British government all along.

To cut a long story short, the Germans abandoned Prize Rules, and fearing their submarines would be sunk by apparently unarmed civilian ships which were in fact heavily armed military ships, which was a justifiable claim, they instead adopted the policy of unrestricted submarine warfare, which allowed any ship to be sunk without warning, with the argument that this was a perfectly legal action when attacking military ships.

Ultimately, U-boats from then on simply sank ships on sight, without warning, as the Germans argued they had no choice, which became a big factor in drawing America into the war, which once again begs the question, was this the actual intention?

I honestly find it fascinating that you can wander our lovely little island and come across fantastic stories like this literally everywhere, and you only have to do a bit of digging to find that one thing will take you to another until you have a most tangled but very interesting web.

Anyway, as I said, we were not going to Thorpe Bassett today, so we turned right and headed across fields towards Wintringham, and after crossing the bridge over a small beck, we were soon walking back down the main street and straight to the car, which was exactly where we had left it under the tree next to the old whitewashed cottages, although now it was considerably more covered in bird poop than it had been that morning, much to Rob's annoyance.

WINTRINGHAM TO GANTON

The sun followed me to Ganton, which is where I met Rob and Chris, and which is also where we left my car. It took us a while to find each other, as we had arranged to meet at the corner where the village began, which in retrospect is probably something of a vague location especially when we all ended up approaching the village from different directions.

I had come from the south on some crazy minor road that led across the tops of the Wolds from Driffield, whereas Chris had approached from the east on the main road and Robin had driven in from the west. There is not much in it distance-wise as to which way had been the best way to go, but obviously, my way had been the best way to go, but there you go.

Anyway, I sat waiting in my car for a while,

and after 10 minutes figured something was amiss. I texted Robin to see if he was dead in a ditch, or worse, had slept in, and he sent a message back saying that he had just pulled up. Getting out of my car, I could see that Robin was mistaken and there was no one around, although I did see some curtains twitching as someone was clearly spying on me and wondering what on earth I was up to at this time of the morning, parked outside of their house and having a good look around.

Seeing no sign of Robin, I wondered if I was in the wrong village, so I walked back to the sign and discovered that I certainly was in Ganton, and I was parked on Woodside Road, information which I passed to Rob. All I got in return was a question mark, as it turns out that he had also pulled into Woodside Road, and he sent me a picture of the road sign to prove it, which puzzled me for a minute because I was stood there and he most certainly was not.

Chris then got involved, texting that he had been waiting for ten minutes and couldn't see either of us, and was asking how long we would be, and I seriously wondered how big this village could possibly be. Jumping back in my car, I figured the only thing to do was to have a drive around the village to see if I could find my lost buddies and to rescue them of course.

I found Rob first, at the wrong end of Woodside Road, whereupon he asked me why I had parked at the wrong end of it, the cheek. He followed me as I continued to circle the village, and not surprisingly we found Chris outside the pub, The Ganton Greyhound, although admittedly he was also parked on yet another corner.

Anyway, we drove down towards the church and left two of the cars there, and jumped into Rob's car for the short drive to Wintringham. The drive only took a few minutes, as we followed the main road almost all of the way, with the hills rising up to the wooded Wolds on our left, and to the Yorkshire Moors on our right. Broken only by some traffic lights at Sherburn, it was non-stop back to our starting point, in what seemed no time at all, yet it was going to take us many hours to walk back.

We dumped the car in the village, and after a quick change, we were off. Doubling back at first, as the path didn't actually go through the village but round it, we were soon caked in mud and trudging through puddles, and it was almost as if we had never been away from the trail.

The sun, which had so promisingly followed me to Ganton, had decided to stay there, so it was under overcast skies that our journey began. I had every possible layer on, as it was probably going to rain at some point, and the cold temperatures also tortured us as we struggled to get going.

I thought it a shame that the path didn't actually go through Wintringham, as it is a very

A WALK ON THE WILD SIDE

pretty little village, but anyway we were soon at the far end of it standing in front of the church, which was St Peter's.

I decided to go in and have a little look while Rob and Chris sat outside, adjusting rucksacks and laces. It was surprisingly light and airy inside, and while looking around I saw an ornately carved poor box, basically a charity collection box, but this one was different because of its age, at around 400 years old. There were all sorts of odd carvings as well, including dragons, which are always cool.

Back outside, the other two had finally managed to tie their laces, bless them, so we continued on our merry way, which was of course uphill. It was gentle at first, as we headed towards a wood, but it soon became much, much steeper, and I wondered how was it that so many of our walks managed to start in this way.

Just before we disappeared into the woods, we stopped to have a look back at the view, which was absolutely awesome even on a dreary day like today. As well as Wintringham immediately below us, it was just possible to make out Thorpe Basset behind it, but much clearer behind that was Rillington, famous for not much other than giving its name to Rillington Place in London, the site of several notorious murders.

Rillington Place is in Notting Hill, but when these murders happened in the 1940s and 1950s, it was not the up-and-coming place that it is today, but was quite frankly a ghetto.

The murderer in question was John Christie. If you don't know the story, there would probably be a disclaimer if you were watching a news broadcast about him, as Christie was basically a psychopath, weirdo, and a generally scary person.

It is thought that he murdered at least eight people, including his own wife Ethel, and it is probably fair to say that he was into necrophilia, as he is reported to have violated several of his victims. He didn't so much as get rid of the bodies either, preferring instead to creatively stash them variously in secret cupboards or under the floorboards or to bury them in the garden.

This would probably have been okay had he lived in Rillington Place until he popped his clogs himself, however, instead he moved house in 1953, and imagine the surprise when the next occupant of the house decided to do a bit of DIY one Sunday, and three bodies fell out of the cupboard. I am being serious here, as that is exactly what happened.

In all fairness, alarm bells should have gone off a couple of years earlier, when one of Christie's tenants, Timothy Evans, was arrested for the murder of his wife and child. In fact, Christie was the killer, after having offered to perform an abortion on Evans' wife, Beryl.

The police did not exactly go all out to investigate this murder, and being of low intelligence, Timothy Evans was induced to confess for the crime, and later on, to the death of his daughter too. He was hanged in 1950, and the truth only came out when bodies started popping out all over Rillington Place after his death.

This particular miscarriage of justice was later a huge influence on the abolition of capital punishment for murder in the UK in 1965, and Evans was later posthumously pardoned, although it was, of course, a little bit late for that unless someone was going to have a go at bringing him back from the dead.

Ironically, Christie was himself executed just a few years after Evans and suffered the exact same fate of death by hanging, at the same location in Pentonville Prison, on the same gallows and with the same executioner, the infamous Albert Pierrepoint. There is a funny story here, as once Christie had been restrained, he is reported to have remarked to Pierrepoint that his nose was itching, to which Pierrepoint replied that he should not worry about it as it wouldn't be bothering him for very long.

Christie was buried within the grounds of Pentonville Prison near to the grave of Timothy Evans, which is surprisingly not in Pentonville but in Islington by the way, so will technically remain locked up for all eternity, or at least until they knock the place down and build a housing estate on it. Evans was granted a royal pardon in 1966 and released from prison, although he was still dead of course. More accurately, his body was exhumed, and he was afforded a more dignified burial in a Roman Catholic Cemetery

On that cheery story, we entered the dark wood that was Deepdale Plantation and followed a track that led us to the north. It was a steep climb up, and we huffed and puffed like the big bad wolf, although we weren't as good looking.

Almost as soon as we entered the wood, Chris decided that he needed to answer a call of nature, though just a quick one he assured us, so we told him that we would carry on walking slowly and he could catch us up in a few moments.

What Chris did not know, however, was that Robin and I had a cunning plan.

As Chris found a suitable tree and then faffed about taking his gloves off and messing with various zips and buttons, Robin and I managed to get a good few yards ahead and were soon out of sight. Once we were sure that Chris could no longer see or hear us, we ventured off the track and hid behind the biggest tree we could find. The idea was to wait for Chris to catch up to this spot, and when he was almost upon us, we would jump out, either screaming at him to run for his life which we hoped would put the fear of God into him or maybe just jump out, making barking noises just after he had passed, thereby facilitating a mild heart attack or something equally funny.

We waited, and waited, and wondered what Chris was doing, though then, of course, we immediately wished we hadn't.

Eventually, you see, after what seemed like a very long time, at least to two childish and impatient grown men hiding behind a tree, we heard a noise, maybe the cracking of a twig or something similar, which suggested Chris might now be approaching.

We hushed our whispers and waited, although we heard no further noise and saw no sign of Chris, though we imagined that at any minute now he would appear in front of us and fall right into our trap.

An incredibly loud voice bellowed from behind us. *What are you up to lads?*

Chris had sneaked around behind us after he had figured out what we were up to, which says a lot about our childish predictability, and had in fact almost given us the heart attacks. I nearly jumped out of my skin, and I think Robin actually went to the toilet as a result, and after a bit of a giggle, we carried on.

We emerged out of the trees on top of a hill that gave wonderful views across the Vale of Pickering and passed through one of the most rustic gates I had ever seen on a national trail. It was made from rough twisted timber and would have been at home on the way into Hogwarts. As well as being beautiful in itself, the view complemented it further, and while it may seem strange to talk of a mere gate in this manner, you really have to see it for yourself.

A round pond to our left was currently accommodating a brown labrador, although I don't think he had necessarily been brown before he had gone in, and if you stooped low to the ground, the little circle of water almost gave the impression of an infinity pool that you see on holiday, though without the blue skies and Pina Coladas, of course.

We left the dog's owner behind as he tried to entice his aquatic animal out of the water, and I don't think he had even noticed us, that focused was he on trying to get his dog back.

Turning east, the sun offered itself tantalizingly through the clouds but ultimately failed to deliver as we followed the edge of the wood at the top of this hill. The views were great, and we could occasionally see through the trees across the whole of the Vale of Pickering, or at least that is how it seemed.

It was an incredibly long and straight path, and we talked about this and that as we went along. Robin and I are in some ways at different ends of the political spectrum, but we have never fallen out over politics. Instead, we simply agree to disagree. In fact, I simply excuse him for being wrong, and he excuses me for being incorrect, and I can never understand why people fall out over such things.

We do, however, also agree on a lot of things, in fact, more things than we would disagree about, and we manage to find common ground on many things, which is actually a lot harder than it sounds in the world of today where people seem to be less tolerant in general, and often choose to live in little echo chambers, where they only read and hear about things that they agree with anyway.

In the field to our right, two hares suddenly startled us from our daydreaming state as they sensed our approach and fled at what seemed to be an impossible speed. They raced across the field and were gone after just a few seconds, after which we changed the subject.

Beyond where the hares had disappeared, there was a campsite which looked to be pretty empty, not surprising given the time of year, although there were one or two caravans and tents occupied by presumably more hardy campers.

Rain began to fall, although it was only light and did not pose any problems, but it did seem to shut us up, as we then proceeded in silence until we came to a road a little further on, and where I immediately knew where I was.

Somewhere down the hill was the small village of West Heslerton, which, if you had been in the market for a village recently, you could have picked up for a cool £20 million. Unfortunately, however, if you are now thinking that, yes, maybe you would like a village, then you have been pipped at the post, as it has since been bought by Count Luca Rinaldo Contardo Padulli di Vighignolo. I certainly hope I spelt his name right because I do not want to get on the wrong side of a reclusive millionaire, or more likely billionaire.

Anyway, not a lot is known about the Count, other than he is, of course, filthy rich, and also that he has good taste in villages because West Heslerton is a truly nice place with a fabulous little pub, but unfortunately, it is just a little too far off our path today to justify a visit.

This is a shame because there is a big old wreck of a stately home there that is literally decaying before everyone's eyes and that is well worth a look at too. West Heslerton Hall was built by Charles Sykes for his daughter in the mid to late 1700s, and is not a bad wedding gift by anyone's standards, and remained an impressive house for the next couple of centuries. Boasting 21 bedrooms, which makes it ideal for parties or games of hide and seek I imagine, it was passed down and sold on over the years, and by the mid-1900s it had found its way into the hands of a lady called Eve Dawnay, who worked hard to retain the character of both the hall and the village. Although Dawnay moved out into a smaller property in the 1980s, she remained much loved and respected by the locals, although the house began to fall into a major state of disrepair after this. It is probably in an even worse state now, and I have seen several pictures taken by so-called urban explorers, and despite its state, it remains an impressive and beautiful old house.

Like I said though, that is not for today, and after a quick uphill walk along the road, we were soon once again heading off into the fields. We ended up going around three sides of a wood before once again finding ourselves heading east, although we were now out in the open and certainly felt an immediate drop in the temperature as a result.

The lack of trees once again gave us fantastic views, of course, and for the next mile and a half, I can confirm that I never once got tired of it. The weather was not great, and the visibility was not perfect, but you could see down into the valley below clearly enough. Various signs of life gave away the presence of people, such as chimneys smoking away in the chill winter air, and the traffic on the main road which seemed to be moving incredibly slowly from way up here, as well as a lone solitary tractor that ploughed its way up and down a field around a mile away at what seemed like a glacial pace.

High above East Heslerton, someone had built some fine-looking camping pods, and I took a leaflet from a small plastic dispenser, on account that this was the sort of place that our wives would like to drag us at some point, although we wouldn't need much dragging, of course. The view here was particularly beautiful, too, and in the distance, we could clearly see the snow-covered hills of the North Yorkshire Moors spreading out across the horizon to the north, and was something we enjoyed for the next couple of miles.

Turning away from the view, the path led us uphill slightly and through a small copse, where we emerged onto a single-track road that looked to lead us gently down a hill.

Turning as it went, we were now heading for Sherburn, and although the slope was gentle at first, we were soon being led more by gravity than by our feet. Young trees lined this busy little road, and every time a car came, we hopped onto the grass verge, which proved to be pretty often.

Almost without exception, we got that little Yorkshire wave from all of the passing car drivers that you don't perhaps get in other places, although I haven't yet been everywhere so what do I know.

Gaps in the trees gave us our last views of the valley below, and soon enough, we were in that valley. The path doesn't quite make it to Sherburn, but we were having a quick diversion there today as we had seen a little shop there as we drove through earlier.

Soon enough, we found ourselves at the traffic lights that had stopped us that morning and which were next to the general store, where we all

A WALK ON THE WILD SIDE

piled in at once to peruse whatever was on offer for us in there.

It was nice just to get out of the cold for a while, so we certainly didn't rush our shopping. I variously picked up a can of coke, but then swapped this for milk, but ultimately got both, and then went to the fridge to see the options. Pork pies were my usual choice, but today I went for a vegetable pasty just to be awkward, and then went to pay.

The young girl on the counter was serving someone already, and I waited patiently behind them while she scanned all the items. There wasn't a great deal, it was just a basket full after all, and it maybe came to around ten pounds, although I wasn't really taking much notice as I was getting my money's worth and reading all of the newspaper headlines for free.

Anyway, the girl told the customer, an older lady, how much her shopping was, at which point the shopper began to slowly, ever so slowly, open her little purse. She then spent the next two days counting out the smallest denominations of coins she could find in there, including some that looked like they had gone out of circulation some centuries before and might even be quite valuable.

To top it off, the lady was short of the required amount by quite a bit, and the girl on the till didn't have much sympathy. After umming and aahing for about an hour, she finally suggested that the old lady put something back, but she didn't have a lot to put back, to be honest.

This had been going on for quite some time, to the point that my food was rapidly approaching its use-by date, so I did the only thing I could do and told the shop assistant that I would pay the difference. She looked at me as if I was an insect crawling up her arm, but then said okay, and I handed over what was only a couple of quid for which the old lady thanked me profusely and then went on her way and left the shop.

When she had gone, I asked the girl on the till if the old lady was a local, and she said that yes, she was. Apparently, she lives in the big house on the corner and does this till trick all the time, which probably explains why she lives in the big house on the corner.

We all bought our little treats and left the shop, and when I did so, I looked to find the so-called big house on the corner so I could go and get my two quid back. This was not exactly an address as such, so I had no idea which one it was, and became resigned to the fact that forevermore I would be two pounds short on my net-worth, and decided to learn from my mistake.

We found a little bench under a tree just near the shop, with what looked like some kind of water pump next to it, though I couldn't get any water out of it so assumed it was just for show. As our buttocks slowly began to freeze to the bench,

A WALK ON THE WILD SIDE

however, we decided it was time to move on and would eat on the move instead. My pasty was incredibly delicious and was soon thoroughly devoured, at which point I decided I had not bought enough food and was still hungry.

My pitiful looks to Robin and Chris worked, and I had soon obtained a mars bar and a penguin, which followed the path of the pasty more or less immediately.

Soon enough we were back at the sign telling us we would now be continuing along the Wolds Way, although we had nearly turned off down an earlier track until Robin noticed that there was no fingerpost there, and once back on the correct path, we could concentrate on knocking those miles off.

Incidentally, although there was no sign of it today, Sherburn is the home of the Great Yorkshire Maze. If you come here in summer, however, then you will find a field full of maize, probably, that has been carefully planned out so as to facilitate the losing of children, in-laws, and other generally annoying people.

For this service, as noble as it is, there is, however, a charge, and quite a substantial one it is too. This is where I see a business opportunity, so if anyone out there actually wants to pay good money to get lost in a field, then why don't you get in touch with me, and I can almost guarantee that we will be lost within the hour.

Anyway, moving on, and the rain that had more or less held off now joined us in quite a liberal fashion. We all retreated under our various hoods and hats in a meagre attempt to stay dry, an action which seemed to once again kill off the conversation almost immediately.

The track was short-lived, and we soon found ourselves on another road, though this one was wider, and as a consequence, busier than the last. Just after a farm that offered kindling at such good rates that I almost considered buying us all a bag, the road split off into two, and we took the left option, which obviously meant that we had to go uphill again.

A sign warned of a 16% hill up ahead of us, at which we all stopped and sighed, mentally searching our rucksacks for stuff that we could discard similar to the likes of a hot air ballooner who finds him or herself heading for power lines.

Unfortunately, I think we all needed pretty much everything we had, and anyway, 16% wasn't so bad we decided.

About 20 minutes later, when we all lay huffing and puffing at the top of the hill like asthmatic donkeys, we decided that 16% was actually all that bad, particularly after just stuffing yourself with a vegetable pasty, a couple of chocolate bars and a pint of milk.

It took us a few minutes to recover before we managed to gather the energy to continue onto the track that led away from the road, at which point we found that we were not even at the top of the hill, but only halfway up.

Luckily, we didn't have to climb any higher just yet, as the path more or less followed the contours of the hill, and by the time we did have to go up a bit more, we had more or less recovered. This uphill stretch was short-lived, too, as we then took off into a wood where we once again immediately found ourselves going downhill.

When we came out of the trees and could once again see across the valley, the darkness of the clouds offered a striking contrast to the intermittent sunshine that was trying to break through, despite the continuing rain. What looked like pig pens dotted the landscape ahead of us, and when we got closer, we discovered that is exactly what they were.

A multitude of hogs of all different sizes eyed us lazily as we passed, with their floppy ears half dangling over their eyes, and I did not need reminding that if one of us happened to drop unconscious into one of their pens, then it is likely that they would have us for supper. You see, it is a fact – pigs eat people, which is only fair when you consider that people eat pigs. You could even call it self-defence.

The mafia has long been aware of this, and are said to have used it on several occasions, as it is a well-known fact that pigs will eat almost anything that they can chew, and have even been known to eat pork on occasions, so bear that in mind whenever you are out walking in the country, and pay particular attention when passing piggies.

A rainbow stood behind us, and a proper look revealed it to be a double rainbow, with the colours clearly visible against the drab background, and as we continued down the hill and turned to the east, the sun finally broke through and with it, the rain vanished.

We came to a track next to a fine old cottage which looked to be very solid and made of stone, and it was only when my eyes had adjusted to the darkness that was the kitchen window that I realised that someone was staring back at me. I waved and moved on, and I am glad to say that whoever was in there waved back and smiled, which is a lot better than calling the police or coming outside with your shotgun and shouting *get off my land*.

There was a house here that was called Dawnay Lodge, and I wondered if this was where Eve Dawnay had ended up when she had abandoned West Heslerton Hall. It was still a very nice house and would have been a lovely place to spend your retirement in if it had been.

On the map, this place was marked as the village of Potter Brompton, but in reality, it was little more than a couple of houses by the looks of it, and we soon left it behind, with the next stop being our last, which was of course Ganton.

It was only a short hop across another field, and we were soon on the road that I had used to drive into Ganton that morning, though this was of course new territory for Robin and Chris who had gone the wrong way round.

The road took us past Ganton Hall, which you could just make out in the distance. It looks like a very nice house, I thought to myself, as I wondered who could possibly afford to live there. The answer to that is Nicholas Wrigley, and while that name might not be immediately familiar to you, you probably have heard of him. He was the chairman of a building company called Persimmon but had to resign due to a backlash after he awarded his CEO, Jeff Fairburn, a £128 million bonus in 2017, an absolutely obscene amount by any standards. I hope they pay their builders equally well; you know, those that actually did all the work, but somehow, I doubt it. I don't think there is any justification for being able to say that someone *earned* £128 million, ever. Earned is not the right word, in my opinion, but what do I know. Anyway, nice house.

The car sat there waiting for us, and we were all pretty happy to get our boots off and plonk ourselves on a seat. Geese flew overhead as we sorted ourselves out, honking all the while relentlessly.

We were soon on our way home, via Wintringham of course, where we bade our farewells and went our separate ways, though in the car beforehand, we talked about how it was kind of sad that we had now almost finished this walk, with only one stage left to go.

Oh well, all good things must come to an end, I guess, and with that, we were done for the day.

GANTON TO FILEY

Today is somewhat of an experiment, as we had arranged to meet at elders newlyweds rally, and no, you did not read that incorrectly. While this may raise some eyebrows, and possibly bring to mind all sorts of bizarre images of pensioners getting up to who knows what, it is, in fact, a location. Allow me to explain.

What Three Words is an app that divides the entire planet into small squares which are 3 metres by 3 metres in size, which is about 10 feet in English, and each square is represented by a random assortment of three words. While we have all been using GPS to get around for a couple of decades now, it is not exactly user friendly to tell your mates to meet you at 53.183N 0.487W, and the words are generally much easier to remember for our feeble human brains.

Similarly, as I can attest to on many occasions, apparently simple instructions such as meet me at the main door, can and often have gone bizarrely wrong, as after an hour of huffing and puffing and being unable to get a good enough phone signal, you are somewhat surprised to find that the stadium, theatre or shopping centre you happen to be at, actually has several dozen what you could call main doors, and of course you have been waiting pointlessly at the wrong one, you idiot. What three words makes all of this redundant, in theory anyway.

To make all of our lives go that much smoother then, some cunning webeneurs came up with what three words to make meeting your buddies that much easier. While an earlier attempt to get a taxi to pick Robin up while we had been walking along the Cleveland Way using what three words proved to be unsuccessful, this was in the early days of the app, and there is probably much more awareness of it now.

Although it allows friends to meet up at an incredibly specific location, and one that usually has quite an easy to remember name, it has also since been adopted by various emergency services worldwide, and it has since been used in England and Australia to actually rescue people.

Although somewhat less critical in that we are not the emergency services and we are not rescuing anyone, the app proves to be successful today, too, and by 9 o'clock, me and Rob had managed to find Chris parked up pretty close to elders newlyweds rally, and we are soon geared up and ready to go. Rob was in my car as we had left his at Filey on the way here, of course. This is clearly a better outcome than arranging to meet at the first corner in the village, which really didn't work out all that well last time.

Interestingly, what three words has been parodied by many, and one of my favourite of these impersonators is what3f**ks. This, as you can probably imagine, splits the world into a similar grid, but gives each one a specific name made up of three swear words. This is probably one step up from the original, and I would love to tell my mates to meet me at ginger cow crap, which is one of the few and mildest examples I could find, yet unfortunately, the app seems to have been pulled.

They needn't have bothered anyway, as what three words gives many funny and humorous examples of places to meet around the world, despite the inventors trying hard to make this not so by excluding all swear words, among many others.

For instance, stiff little finger will see you meet, perhaps quite appropriately considering your poorly digit, at a hospital in Bozeman, Montana. Don't fancy that one? How about credit card denied, something I have encountered often being a poor and struggling writer, which will see you meet up in the middle of nowhere, although still somewhere in Ontario, Canada. Watch out for bears, though, as this is not far from Polar Bear Provincial Park, which is somewhere I am loosely familiar with, and is a place that can be quite bad for your health.

If you fancy shame without regret, then you need to head to chilly Oslo in Norway, and finally, forget previous husband is, perhaps appropriately, in the middle of the South Atlantic, so good luck with that.

Anyway, it is time to walk, and the weather gods appear to be shining on us today. Sunshine is trying to break out from behind the cloud, although it may well be fighting a losing battle, but it is dry and not too cold, and with that, we are off.

Ganton itself is a pretty little village, with old white-washed cottages lining each side of the road. There is also a bubbling brook on one side, with neat little bridges leading to each doorway, which all look very picturesque. The place is noted for little else, although it has quite a nice golf course that somehow once managed to host the Ryder Cup in 1949. I thought this to be a joke when I first heard the story, but I can assure you I have done all of the due diligence, and unlikely as it sounds, it is indeed very true. And there is more.

We have to remember that Britain in 1949 was not the land of plenty that we enjoy today. Wartime rationing had continued, and there was much that you simply could not get at the time, but the Americans had a cunning plan. Their captain, Ben Hogan, who incidentally did not play in the cup as he was still recovering from a car accident, was aware of the dire food situation in England, and therefore quite sensibly decided to bring all of their own food with them.

He didn't mess about, either. In his little hamper, he packed 600 steaks, 12 sides of ribs along with a dozen hams, and chucked in a dozen boxes of bacon for good measure. When the British press found out about this, it all made more headlines than the actual golf, which clearly annoyed Hogan. On the 13 September 1949, the St Petersburg Press printed a story about the affair, and Hogan complains vigorously at all the attention being put on the matter, saying he is *sick and tired of all the harping on.* He complains that the British press never printed what Lord so-and-so had for dinner every night and that the food was intended not just for the American golfers, but for their wives and girlfriends who had accompanied them, as well as for entertaining the British golfers and their wives and girlfriends too. What is most surprising from this is clearly the fact that the golfers had taken both their wives and girlfriends, whereas my grandad always told me that never the twain shall meet.

Anyway, the better nourished Americans ultimately won the 1949 Ryder Cup, which is not all that surprising when you think about it.

We followed a path that led out of the village and were soon in a field somewhere behind St Nicholas' Church. Stopping for a moment to enjoy the views, we could see a vast swathe of the Vale of Pickering to the north, with the last of the Yorkshire Wolds rising steeply behind us. We would be following the edge of the Wolds today and should get some more good views, and we would first be heading uphill to Staxton Wold Farm, and then on to the RAF base with the same name. From there, a series of twists and turns would take us across and around a few hills and dales, passing north of Hunmanby and straight through Muston. From there, it was a relatively short walk into Filey, and up to the Brigg where this walk would finish.

Unfortunately, our direction of travel soon turned to take us straight up the steep hills to our south, and I was soon out of breath. I expect Robin and Chris felt the same, and as a consequence our conversation seemed to die abruptly, almost before it had even started.

This was hard going so early on in the day, and I immediately regretted not having done any stretching or warming up exercises today, although it was clearly too late now. Thankfully, after this rather rude interruption, another turn saw us once again walking on a relatively flat path, which allowed us to get our breath back somewhat.

A tractor was ploughing the field immediately behind us, and thousands of gulls were following behind it, obviously enjoying whatever they were finding in the upturned soil. For a minute, I felt spots of rain on my face, but looking around there seemed no real possibility of any kind of shower, as the sky had continued to brighten since we had set off.

Another turn put us at the bottom of yet another steep climb, and as we once again went quiet, we trudged our way up, which was now made even harder by walking through slick wet mud that stuck to our boots and shoes. My feet felt suddenly heavy and made walking much harder than you would expect from what is in effect quite a small amount of the stuff, so I tried to scrape some of it off on the grass. This helped a little bit, and as I carried on, hugging the edge of the field and trying to avoid the sloppiest bits, it was a losing battle, and I was soon enough once again caked in the stuff.

This continued more or less until we got to the main road at Staxton Hill Farm, and from here on, we had the luxury of a proper track to walk on. Once again, the long grass helped us to clean our boots and shoes before we continued, and I for one felt that I could now fly having gotten rid of the gloopy stuff with the help of a stick.

The track was long, and in the distance, we could see the various towers and domes of RAF Staxton Wold. As we neared, a white van came from the base and parked up on the perimeter. I can't imagine for one minute they were watching us, but you never know.

The base has an interesting history and has been used as one type of lookout or another for hundreds of years. There was a beacon up here from around 300 AD, and the first actual radar installation was built here just before the Second World War. Amazingly, the government almost never managed to get the thing built, as the original landowner refused to sell, but with the imminent threat of Herr Hitler, he finally saw sense, and the site opened in early 1939, which was just in time of course.

It has been operating as a radar station ever since, and according to the RAF, being the only original site still in use, it is, in fact, the oldest continuously serving radar station in the world. Who knew? Not me.

The guys in the van eye us warily, and a quick wave as we pass elicits no response. I'm sure they are very nice people, who are just doing their job, but they seem miserable doing it. They are, however, protecting the site, which is, in turn, protecting us, I guess, and also protecting the surrounding landscape in more ways than one.

As well as watching out for pesky Russian planes testing our defences, this radar site has also protected the countryside from what some people would call the blight of wind turbines. Whether you love them or hate them, they certainly seem to be everywhere nowadays, but not so much around here you may notice. The reason is that the turbines can often interfere with radar systems, and generally whenever someone announces that they are going to build a wind farm anywhere, one of the first considerations is its impact of the defence of the country.

For years, RAF Staxton Wold was an obstacle in building a wind farm at Fraisthorpe, just a few miles down the coast past Bridlington. The local people seemed to object too, and there was literally an objection for every day of the year, with 365 letters being sent in to oppose the plans. Petitions were signed against the turbines, and even renowned artist David Hockney got involved, who painted many scenes around these parts, saying that a wind farm would deface the area.

Ultimately, though, RAF Staxton Wold gave the go-ahead to the wind farm when they upgraded the radar system here to one that would not be affected as much as the old one would have been by any big spinny things. When the Ministry of Defence dropped their objections, the wind farm went ahead, and that was the end of that.

A path led south and away from the base, and as I looked over my shoulder, I saw the van disappearing back into the base, which left me somewhat bemused. I'm not sure what threat they thought we were exactly, but they had clearly driven out so they could have a good look at us, though they maybe just did it for fun or perhaps because they were bored.

Walking into some trees and slightly down a hill, the path got muddy once again, and we followed this heavily rutted lane for a few hundred yards before we turned abruptly left and headed across the fields of Flixton Wold.

Whatever crops had grown here were long gone, and just stubble remained, presumably awaiting the plough that we saw earlier. The ground was at least firmer and easier to walk on, and there was even a well-trodden path that was easy to make out.

A huge German Shepherd was bounding towards us, and for a moment I had a feeling of fear, but then realized that I was a faster runner than Robin, so if push came to shove, it would be him that became a dog's dinner and not me. We needn't have worried, though, as the owner was not far behind and she soon had the dog on a lead.

I imagined that it was one of those gentle giant dogs, but then Gail, for that was her name she said, told us that she put Blade on a lead as he has a tendency to nibble people and he can be a bit vicious. I'm pretty sure she saw my facial expression change and my eyebrows defy gravity, but she didn't say anything if she did. At least she was being honest.

All the while, the dog just sat there while

we chatted, and he did not seem in the slightest to be a dangerous type of beast, so maybe she was just being over-cautious. Anyway, she told us that the path up ahead was a bit slippy, at least until we got to the next road, and said the cows were a bit jumpy in the next field. I silently pondered whether or not the cows were perhaps a bit jumpy because she had just taken Blade through their field and he had scared the heebie-jeebies out of them, which would certainly make sense.

The cows were indeed a bit jumpy and were very vocal as we passed through their field. They refused to move out of the way, and we were forced to go right through the middle of the herd, although there was a pretty big gap for us to get through. I noted there were no calves, which can make mothers particularly protective and unpredictable, and I also made sure that I was in the middle, with Robin up ahead of me and Chris just behind. This was my cunning plan to at least be the last to die.

As it was, nobody died, and the moody cows were, if you pardon the pun, simply that. This part of the walk was particularly scenic, with some unspoiled dales just to our south which were very pleasing to the eye, and which helped explain why David Hockney enjoyed painting the area so much.

Passing the wonderfully named Humble Bee Farm, which sat nestled in the snug of a small valley, we noticed several yurts and cabins and imagined them to be glamping type pods, which is the only type of camping my wife likes. Robin agreed, as his better half is the same and neither do well in a tent, but they might like to come here, so when I win the lottery, it will definitely be on the list of things to do.

We crossed the main road and could see a small clump of trees, marking the spot of Sharpe Howe Round Barrow. This is, in fact, an ancient grave, and where William Greenwell excavated eight bodies in the late 1800s.

William Greenwell, or Canon Greenwell as he is also known, was a Victorian amateur archaeologist of mixed repute as we heard earlier, although he was held in extremely high esteem during his lifetime. He was born to a family with money and grew up on the family estate that contained the site of Longovicium Roman Fort, which sparked his initial interest in archaeology. His obituary in *Nature* magazine tells us, among other things, that he was elected as a fellow of the Society of Antiquities in 1868, though he didn't bother to turn up to be admitted until some seven years later, and was elected as a fellow of the Royal Society a decade later in 1878. Lastly, it says that he was pretty good at fishing, too.

As well as digging up the mound currently in front of us, Greenwell is also noted for working on Danes Graves, where if you will remember, he worked with John Mortimer of Fimber. Danes

Graves is an iron age site a few miles to the south of here, and Greenwell also worked at the much more famous Grime's Graves in Norfolk. The Canon title, by the way, comes from the fact that he was for a long time the Canon of Durham Cathedral, which is perhaps one of the more noble aspects of his life.

Greenwell's archaeological method is certainly open to question, however. After working at Danes Graves, the landowner described Greenwell as *reckless, careless and indecent*, and complained that he had not even bothered to refill any holes he had dug, leading him to forever ban all further excavation on the site. One success from the site, though, is the Bronze age chariot that was unearthed, along with the chieftain it was buried with and his charioteer who was presumably killed purely to accompany his master into the afterlife. This is also thought to be a grave of the Parisii people who we heard about earlier, and who lived in this region for many years, and what is left of the chariot, which it must be said is not a lot, can now be found gathering dust in the Yorkshire Museum in York.

Greenwell cheekily sold on much of what he had found on other peoples' land, and became rich as a consequence, to the extent that he eventually had enough money to buy back the family estate where he had grown up, which must have been a substantial fortune it has to be said. He sold much of his collection to John Pierpont Morgan, better known of course as J.P. Morgan, millionaire and philanthropist, who eventually donated it to the British Museum.

There is not a lot to look at today, it is really just a bit of raised earth with some trees growing on top of it, but these barrows are all over the place around here, and who knows, one of them might still contain some incredible treasures. There is another one a few miles to the south, the much better named Willy Howe, which Greenwell also vandalised at some point, which has various fairy tales attached to it. When passing, one man was said to have entered a hole in the side of the mound and was given a drink by the fairies he found inside. The cup was made of gold, and when the young man realised this, he ran off with it and was chased by the fairies. There was also said to be a treasure chest buried within the mound, which you never know, might explain Greenwell's riches.

A short stroll along the road to the south soon saw us turn off once more, this time following a grassy track wedged in between two farmer's fields, and with the odd tree dotting the route. Almost immediately we met a couple of hikers coming the other way, and they looked as if they were camping as they went judging by the size of their backpacks, which I considered madness in these colder months.

They were Gregg and Charlie, and they were indeed camping out they told us while walking the

Centenary Way. They had started that very morning from Filey, which is exactly where we would be finishing in just a few hours. When I asked them if they often camped out in the depths of winter, they confirmed that yes, they did, the fools. Wishing them well, we were soon on our way, and although I was looking forward to my nice warm bed tonight, I was kind of envious of what they were doing, especially as they had just started out and would enjoy the next few days walking and camping when we would all be back at work.

We were soon going downhill, first just slightly but then the path became quite steep, and after dropping down into what was Camp Dale, we then had to trudge straight back up the other side of it. We followed the top of the valley as it twisted south, all the time looking down on hundreds of noisy and messy sheep, and after half a mile or so, we descended the hill to the valley bottom, causing the sheep to scatter as we walked through their flock.

As the valley split into two, we turned north into Stocking Dale, though had we been walking the Centenary Way, it is here that we would have headed south instead. I had thought that we would have shared the same path for the rest of the journey, especially when you consider that both routes finish in the same place, but they do in fact follow different routes, and only re-join as you enter Filey.

The walk up Stocking Dale was pleasantly

different to the other dales we had been through. Trees offered a welcome change in scenery and also provided a bit of shelter from the wind. Although it was not that strong today, it was still noticeable, so we appreciated any available shelter whatsoever. The gradient was gentle, and the track was good, which made this perhaps one of the easier places we had walked today, but I wondered if this was psychological being that we were nearly at the end of the walk.

A line of trees greeted us, and a sign pointed to our right, and we found ourselves skirting along what turned into a long, thin wood. It is exactly here that I missed a step, and in doing so went head over heels into the mud.

Immediately I felt a pain shooting up my leg, and for one awful minute, I wondered if I had broken something. Robin & Chris were laughing, and Robin was pulling out his camera, and being honest, I would not expect anything less. I often have laughed when the boot has been on the other foot, so to speak, and I have often done the same as Robin, reaching form my camera while shouting *don't move*, hoping to get the perfect shot.

I think they both saw the look on my face, though, and after getting the picture, both literally and figuratively, they came over to help me. The pain was in my right leg, at the back, and led down all the way to my ankle. I'm guessing it was a nerve that was hurting, and having a history of sciatica in that leg, I can only presume I had agitated an old injury.

Robin and Chris helped me up, and I decided to try and walk it off, but after a few steps, the pain became intolerable, and I had to stop again. I told the others to leave me here to die and to go on in order to save themselves, but Robin refused on the grounds of too much paperwork, and also he would have to answer to my wife, Leeanne.

Within a minute, Robin had dropped his backpack and extracted his first aid kit. A couple of ibuprofens were offered, which I gratefully accepted, and Robin asked me if I would prefer deep-heat or ibuprofen gel. I would have preferred a Jack Daniels, but chose the latter, nonetheless.

It was a good job there was no one around as I dropped my trousers to apply the gel to the back of my leg. Robin and Chris both refused to rub it in, quoting Meat Loaf himself when they said they would do anything, but they wouldn't do that, so I was left to struggle while trying to get to those hard-to-reach spots that we all have.

Obviously, this is when a couple of hikers came around the corner, both older females of course, and as I struggled to my feet and tried to pull my trousers up, I lost my balance and ended up once more in the mud, with my trousers once again around my ankles, more or less.

Luckily, they weren't prudes, and shouted across to me, inquiring whether I was having some difficulty there. Robin told them he would give me a hand, at which point he started clapping, and I remember thinking that with mates like these, who needs enemies.

Strangely, the ladies never stopped to chat but wandered off giggling to themselves about the muddy idiot back there. I managed to get my trousers up, after which I had a good stretch. I could feel the sticky gel on the inside of my trousers, and it felt horrible, and normally I would have let it dry a bit before putting any item of clothing back on, but today I obviously had no choice.

Robin asked if I wanted a minute, but I decided to just keep moving, and in retrospect, this was probably the best decision. It was still incredibly painful, but after around half an hour, I could feel a marked difference, and it felt like my leg had loosened up a fair bit.

Chris asked me if I wanted to finish at the next road, something I seriously considered, but I knew I wanted to go on by the time we got there. Although it was pretty painful, it was clearly not a serious injury. I also knew that it would probably be weeks before I could get back up here to finish the walk if I stopped now. As it was only a handful of miles before we finished, I reckoned I could make it.

We came to the main road at a farm, where a sign announced you could get fresh farm eggs from happy chickens, and I wondered who had done the survey and how impartial they had really been.

The path continued on the other side of the road across a thankfully pretty dry field, and we were soon going slightly downhill towards Muston, which we could see off to the east, and beyond it was Filey and the North Sea.

Joining the road into the village, we initially had enough grass verge to walk on, though this petered out somewhat until we got into the village itself. Taking advantage of a wooden bench with some dead flowers at either end, we had a quick rest, and Chris pulled out a last bag of Haribos, which we all happily munched on.

We were forced to take a second break too, when after a couple of twists and turns, we stumbled, literally in my case, upon the Ship Inn, and decided to invest some of our hard-earned money into the local economy. It was an investment that paid dividends too, as we enjoyed a nice pint of ale while sat around a wonky picnic bench that moved every time someone breathed. As an added bonus, I think the beer acted as a kind of pain relief.

As we all sat there shivering yet still enjoying our pint, across the road was a wooden signpost that appeared to have been built on the base of what was once an old cross. This cross had long since vanished as far back as 1892 when a Bulmer's guide said a wooden sign stood there even then. This same guide also told of some mysterious graves found in the village, which were said to be ancient. Quarrying had revealed the graves, several of them apparently, which consisted of circular holes cut straight into the rock. Bodies had been placed in the holes which had then been backfilled with clay, which all sounds very mysterious and quite frankly, spooky.

We soon finished off our pints and began to move off just as we really began to feel the cold which had crept over us while we were still. My leg was as stiff as anything once again, but after 10 minutes or so it began to loosen up. The road twisted and turned through the village, passing All Saint's Church, followed by some quaint cottages before a swift left turn led us up a small hill and through somebody's garden.

It wasn't really someone's garden of course, but it looked like it. Passing down the side of a field full of tiny horses, we were soon out into the open countryside once again, and on the last leg of our long walk to Filey, or at least we thought we were. Going through a gate and cutting our way through an overgrown hedge jungle style, with both of my walking sticks, I nearly had a heart attack when a lone truck thundered by at around 60 miles an hour. This is exactly the same moment that I was about to step onto a main road and I reckon I was only about an inch from death. I had been that focused on bashing the nettles out of the way, that I just did not notice the road.

Carefully looking left and right, there now appeared to be a constant stream of traffic, alternating first from one way, and when that cleared, there would be vehicles coming from the other direction. It was so annoying, and it seemed as if the traffic was deliberately waiting for one side to clear before blocking you the other way, and it was ages before we finally threw caution to the wind and dashed across the road with a complete disregard for our own safety when we were given just a tiny break in the traffic.

I will swear on anything that the car coming towards us actually speeded up as well, but the joke would have been on him if he had hit us. First of all, chubby hikers can do serious damage to any modern motor car, which are built with crumple zones that are designed to be squashed when hitting forty-something fat blokes. Second, I'm sure the rozzers would have had something to say had he mown us down. So, the last laugh would have been on us. He would have been arrested and lost his no-claims bonus, while we would just be dead.

Filey was ahead of us across the fields, and we went from farmers field to housing estate with just a single step when we emerged onto a little track that led from Filey Dam to the main road. The place was positively buzzing today, and after a few minutes we were surprised to come across a traffic jam in this tiny little seaside town, but soon discovered that it was due to a train passing through the level crossing up ahead.

As we waited for the barriers to lift, we could see the small train station just to our right, in front of which was a model of a small steam engine. A train stood at the platform in the station, the one we were waiting for to pass us as it happened, and after a few moments, it began to move off, passing us on its way north.

We continued on through the town, not really sure where we were going but just trying to head to the centre, and after a while, we were definitely very much among a throng of busy shops. Almost by instinct, we tracked down a local butcher and all piled in for a quick treat. Pork pies were the order of the day; I went for pork and apple, as did Chris, and Robin went for pork and black pudding.

We munched on our little snacks as the road dropped down towards the beach, with the sea now firmly in sight.

Stopping at an overlook just above the beach, we enjoyed the expansive views, taking in our final destination to the north at Filey Brigg, and to the south, we could just make out the white cliffs of Bempton disappearing in the distance.

We walked north, through fairly big crowds of beachgoers, which surprised me in such cold weather, and we figured that most of them were just out for a walk, which is also of course why we were there.

A WALK ON THE WILD SIDE

Heading up the hill towards the country park, we almost didn't want to finish, but on cue, it began to rain just as we approached the headland that was the Brigg, and as we got to the marker that signalled the end of the walk, the rain became so torrential that we soon turned tail and ran for the car which we had left nearby.

Chucking our stuff quickly in the boot and grabbing a change of footwear, we soon had the engine running to warm us up, and we then began the short drive back to Ganton for the other car. After that, it was time to go home.

CONCLUSION

Although this walk had not been the longest, it was certainly one of the more interesting, with many fascinating places along the way. From learning all about airship disasters and the role the area had to play in the story of airships at the beginning, along with the extra link in this area through Margaret Lyon, plus the beautiful views over the Humber estuary, as well of course as the majestic Humber Bridge, particularly as seen from underneath, we had been given a great introduction to the area.

The rather unlikely story of the stolen Roman mosaic had certainly been unexpected, as had the amazing and partly true story of the famous highwayman Dick Turpin, although the rolling dales and dry valleys of the Wolds had not. Swin Dale had been another highlight, offering a tranquil walk through an isolated valley, and had been almost immediately followed by the interesting history of Goodmanham and the Parisii, as well as by the beautiful park of Londesborough.

We'd had a great night and a great meal in Millington, and had then encountered some of the most beautiful unspoilt dales we had ever seen as we walked between Huggate and Fridaythorpe. Thixendale had rounded off day four almost perfectly, apart from nearly being squashed by a car of course, but looking back on that we can laugh about it now. Interestingly, I had personally found this part of the countryside to be much wilder than I had imagined anywhere around here could possibly be.

A fortuitous wrong turn then led us to the beautiful Birdsall Estate, and although it added a few miles to the journey, it added in much more valuable ways too. Just after this, the gorgeous Deepdale then coaxed us into Wharram Percy, which almost stands frozen in time and seems to belong to another age, which it probably does, to be honest, and it is amazing that so much is known about it, which is, of course, a result of it being studied relentlessly for most of the twentieth century.

Wintringham had proven to have some amazing history links to history, particularly regarding the otherwise unknown story of the first submarine ever sunk and its captain George Francis Cholmley who came from the area.

The views along the next stretch, basically all the way from Wintringham to Ganton and somewhat beyond this too, were simply to die for. This is one stretch that I will probably be doing again in the warmer months, just to have another look at the beautiful Vale of Pickering which stretches for as far as the eye can see and to the North Yorkshire Moors.

And finally, Filey. In my mind, this is one of the simplest and nicest of the coastal resorts in England. Under-stated, yet an absolute gem of a place to finish a walk, which probably explains why the Cleveland Way also starts and finishes here, at the impressive Filey Brigg, and quite frankly I can't think of any better place to finish.

HISTORY WALKS

Paul has spent years wandering all over the north of England, finding out about the unusual and often hidden histories that surround us all, and has put pen to paper to share everything he has learned. Join him to discover the secrets that are quite simply all around us. These books offer interesting accounts of our heritage and our landscapes, and can be read in absolutely any order.

54 Degrees North

Drawing a straight line across England at a latitude of exactly 54 degrees and walking along it as close as he can, join Paul as he sets out to learn about this tiny strip of the country and its history including events, people and places. Starting on the east coast in Yorkshire, and somehow ending up in Lancashire, he encounters murderers, film stars, witches and more, all linked in more ways than you might imagine. Discover what links York with Lancaster, and what an alien has to do with Victorian bridges. Learn about the blind man that built many of our roads and the boffins at Aldermaston that wanted to drop a nuclear bomb on them. This is a ramble across our beloved little island that unearths all sorts of unexpected tales and weaves them together in a narrative like no other.

Rambling On

If you're planning on doing the Cleveland Way, or just fancy a bit of a laugh, this could be the book for you! Join Paul as he navigates 109 miles along the Cleveland Way and around the North Yorkshire Moors. Starting in Helmsley on the wettest day of the year, he thinks it can't get worse, but then Storm Francis comes along. Accompanied by his good friend Rob, who carries most of the gear and does most of the cooking, they get lost, sunburned, blistered, and blown away. Learn about pirates, inventors and famous people along the way as Paul rambles on in more ways than one, and find out about the unluckiest house in Yorkshire, all set against the backdrop of the Coronavirus pandemic. And if you want to know what Mick Hucknall has to do with Whitby, and learn about a modern day sailor who stole his own boat, read on...

Coast To Coast

Join Paul as he follows in the great Alfred Wainwright's footsteps on one of the world's best known and most popular walks. Taking in beautiful valleys, misty moors, lovely lakes and pleasing plains, find about about the literal and spiritual highs and lows of this 192-mile walk from St Bees to Robin Hood's Bay, all told in a flowing, candid and light-hearted story. Delving into the history as he goes along, this book will make you want to follow in his footsteps yourself, or if you have already done the Coast to Coast, you will want to grab your shoes and do it again. Mysterious monsters, funny facts and famous figures await. Who knew that there could be so much history attached to this walk. Bridges built for lovers, amazing stories of pirates, devastating murders, stone circles, plots to blow the lake district sky high and ghost stories are all amusingly told against the backdrop of the walk itself. Paul and his friends spend two weeks tracing Wainwrights footsteps in search of an England of old, one that may not have changed as much as you would expect. Faced with challenges from the weather, from themselves and from other hikers, they get drenched, sunburned and lost, all in equal proportions, and time and again are forced to hide in pubs. Will they make it? Read on to find out ...

Hadrians Wall

Join Paul on an epic walk along one of the most famous and interesting walks in the world - Hadrian's Wall. Find all about its history, both ancient and modern, and learn about the people that have tried to destroy it as well as the people that have tried to save it.

This walk covers a lot more than just the wall, though. Find out which king carried around a human arm for luck and learn about one of the most famous spy-swaps in history. But if it's wall you want, find out where to see the longest, the tallest, the best bits and the rudest bits!

Stretching across the north of England, walking the wall sees Paul and the gang enjoy leisurely long summer days tramping across country encountering all sorts of unexpected delights. Spending the week under canvas, they battle the British weather, get fleeced by the locals, and get blisters thrown in for good luck. This book gives a delightful history of the wall, as well as an amusing account of a walk along it, all told in a friendly and light-hearted manner that will make you smile.

Printed in Great Britain
by Amazon